Becoming a Vessel for God's Glory

Mathew E. Tamin

Copyright © 2005 by Mathew E. Tamin

ISBN 0-7414-2679-X

Published by:

INFIの)ITY
PUBLISHING.COM

1094 New DeHaven Street, Suite 100
West Conshohocken, PA 19428-2713
Info@buybooksontheweb.com
www.buybooksontheweb.com
Toll-free (877) BUY BOOK
Local Phone (610) 941-9999
Fax (610) 941-9959

Printed in the United States of America

Printed on Recycled Paper

Published August 2005

Acknowledgments

I want to thank my family. My parents Fidelis and Patricia Bomba for their love, support, encouragement, and spiritual guidance. My grandmother, Constance and Antoinette, Dominic, and Jr. Thanks for being there for me.

Wayne Williams (a.k.a. Brother Wayne), you showed me how to be a man of God. You encouraged, loved, and supported me in everything I did. Much love to you and your family.

Jack Redmond, Dr. David Ireland, Pastor Marlinda Ireland, Dr. Hose Melendez, Dr. Morgan Laury, Ken Wolpin, Gloria Sutton, Weslor Cadeau, Pastor Derrick Greene, Sis. Vanessa Turner, Sis. Molly Kelly, Apostle Black and his wife Pastor Evelyn, Pastor Winston Christian and his wife Sis Glynis Christian, Raul Barriera, Bro. Elvis Ndengi, Pastor Joseph Rosa, Chris Timmons, Mr. Bryan, Ms. Books, Ms. Jenkins, Ms. Wallace, Prof. Mary Zigorsky, Daniel Mercado, William Lane, Solange Auguraud, My awesome group in Social Psychology Class (Danny, Steven, Collen, Christy, Sujan, Megan, Jessica, Teresa, Jennifer, Amanda, Rob, Kim, Valerie, and Rosemary) Andre Robinson, Catrina Davelos, Dennis Dosantos, Chris White, you taught me what it means to give cheerfully. Much love to you. Grace Villard, you encouraged, prayed, loved, and cared for me. You were there for me through my difficulties. Words cannot express how much I appreciate that. I love you mom. Stanley Dez, thanks for your support, encouragement, and prayers. You are always going to be my boy for life. I love you man. Steven Reeves, I appreciate and will never forget the times we walked to school together in the cold, rain, and snow. You are a true friend. You have always been there for me to love, support, and encourage me. Much love to you and your family.

Minister Quwan Ellis, thanks you for all your prayers. You were there to listen and encourage me. I appreciate that. You have shown me what God can do to those who are obedient to Him. Keep up the great work.

Dedication

Holy, worthy, and mighty is the Lord Almighty God. This book is dedicated to God the Father, God the Son, and God the Holy Spirit.

Contents

To contact the author, please visit his website:

www.mathewtamin.com

Introduction

When I was eight years old, I accepted Jesus as my Lord and savior. After I accepted Him, I had dreams and divine revelations that changed the rest of my life. A couple of days after getting saved, Jesus revealed Himself to me in the flesh. When I looked at Him, I saw the holes in his hands where He was nailed and His side where He was pierced. That was just the beginning of the revelations.

As a child, I remember saying to God, "God, I will serve you for as long as I live." When I was two years of age, prophetic words were prophesied about what God was going to do in my life. At age eleven, a pastor prophesied to me about the awesome things God was going to do in my life, how He would use me to preach the Gospel all over the world. At the time, I did not understand what he meant.

My parents made sure that I went to church even when I did not feel like going. I dreaded going to church sometimes because it was too long. Church started at 9 a.m. and did not end until 6 p.m. To make matters worse, we had to come back for evening service. My dad drove the church van, which meant we were the first to get to church and the last to leave. Oh, how I dreaded those days!

I grew up in a rough urban neighborhood where you earned your respect by being a drug dealer rather than by being educated. It was an environment where most of the kids ended up on the streets, dead, in gangs, or locked up. I watched in horror at the percentages of kids that graduated high school and went to college (extremely low), and wondered if I was going to end up like that. It was hard to stay saved in an environment where everything and everyone around you seemed to be negative. Most of the kids professed to be "saved" but their lifestyle did not reflect Christ.

It was hard to have a dream in a place where most of the kids' goal was to be "respected on the street" rather than to have a better life. In them midst of all this, I was persuaded that God had a better plan for my life and He would not let me end up the way others did. I was a young man with a dream; a dream to become somebody; to go to college and get an education; a dream to change the world into a better place.

By the time I finished high school, I had had more encounters with God. Because of them, I was encouraged to write this book. However, after starting college the following year, I had to put the project on hold in order to focus on my education.

This book is about how God kept me during the dark ages in my life. By writing it, I hope to encourage and educate others who might be going through (or know of someone who is going through) what I went through. I did not have anyone to help and encourage me during those painful times. However, I thank God for giving me the opportunity to go through it because now I can help someone else who is going through a similar situation. I learned at a very early age the importance of applying the word of God in my life.

I want to let everyone who will listen know that God has not forgotten about you. Regardless of what situation you find yourself in, hold on to Jesus and do not give up. He will rescue you. God is not a respecter of persons. God is not man that He should lie nor a son of man that He should repent. He does not care about your academic credentials, or how much money you have or do not have in the bank. All He wants is someone who is available for Him to show His glory through. God is not concerned about your ability, but your availability.

If life's problems have you discouraged and your situation seems bad, or if you need some encouragement and want to get closer to God and let Him use you, this is the perfect book for you. However, if you are looking for fiction and hype, then I urge you to stop reading. Everything I said is true. I did not make anything up. The revelations and prophesies came from God not me. I am only a vessel being used for His Glory.

I share stories that some of the closest people in my life have never heard. At times, some of the stories might be funny and make you laugh, while other times they will bring sadness and make you cry.

I address real issues, issues that churches need to address even though they are afraid to. Issues such as lust, masturbation, and pornography. With the technology available to us, especially the Internet, God's people are struggling with these things. Since the advent of the Internet in 1969, access to disturbing images has continually increased. Although the Internet has been very helpful in some ways, it has also been very hurtful.

I will take you in a systematic process through the steps the Holy Spirit took me through in order to become free and stay free of any spiritual bondage I can relate to being in bondage because I, too, needed deliverance. Now I am free because of the Blood of the Lamb.

I grappled with pornography, masturbation, and lust. I knew the Bible said, "Greater is He [Jesus] that is in me than he [Satan] that is in the world" but because of feeding my flesh and not my spirit, it was easier for he that is in the world to be greater than He that was already in me.

When you feed your flesh, you reap the fruits of the flesh—lust, pornography, masturbation, and other things. However, when you feed your Spirit, you reap the fruits of the Spirit—love, joy, peace, patience, kindness, goodness, faithfulness, gentleness and self-control. Start feeding your spirit so that you will not fulfill the lust of the flesh.

It is sad to know that many Christians get their information from everywhere else but the church. It is time for churches all over the world to start taking responsibility. If they do not, this generation, as well as others, is heading towards destruction.

I have a burden and passion in my heart for the young people, to let them know that the Lord wants to use them regardless of where they come from, for He is concerned about their hearts.

When I look around today, I see many young people called to the ministry but are not walking according to their calling. Many people are running away from God instead of running to God. The word of God says, "For I know the plans I have for you, says the Lord, plans of peace and not of evil, to give you a future and a hope". (Jer. 29:1). God wants to give you a future and hope. God wants you to know that *"Before* I formed you in the womb I knew you." God knew you before anyone else did. He is the only One that has the keys to your destiny. Trust Him to guide you in every aspect of your life.

I hope that you will read this book with an open heart and mind. I hope it will make you more passionate about the things of God.

To Mathew from God the father:

"You will help defeat the devil for Me and my Son Jesus will help you. You shall establish My kingdom. I will be your God and you shall be My people. To have Me come and live in you."

Chapter 1

My life is in your hands

Sometimes in life, God allows us to go through certain situations, and often we do not understand why. Life can be complicated when everything around seems to be contrary to what you believe. However, when you learn to trust God, in His timing, all things will work for your good. Sadly, too many people give up before they get their breakthrough. Regardless of what you are going through, DO NOT give up, but keep fighting.

A word of Hope and Encouragement

Say to those who are fearful-hearted, be strong, do not fear! Behold, your God will **come** with vengeance, with the recompense of God; He will **come** and **save** you (Is. 35:4).

Rough Neighborhood

I grew up in Orange, New Jersey, a predominantly black neighborhood filled with potheads and drug dealers. The crime rate was high. There was always a new story about someone being shot, killed, or stabbed. Not the kind of place you would want your child to live. Most of my classmates were either in gangs or getting in trouble with the law. However, this is where I lived.

It was rough growing up in a place where there seemed to be no hope. A place where the only hope you had for a better life was either sports or selling drugs.

As I watched in horror, most of the kids I knew were turning to drugs and gangs for hope. There I was, stuck in the middle of two worlds: Jesus or the streets.

The kids that were involved in gangs were the primary people starting the fights. They knew they had other gang members to support them when something bad happens. They used weapons, hurting anyone who messed with them. The major gangs were the bloods and the cribs. These two gangs did not like each other. Whenever there was a fight, it was primarily between these two gangs. The police had to get involved in order to stop the fights. Because of this, several students lost their lives. Sadly, I knew most of them.

The Park

After school, I usually went to the park with my basketball and stayed there for the rest of the evening. Sometimes I found myself in trouble because it was not advisable to stay in the park at night. People had sex, drank, and sold drugs during the evening hours.

My parents always locked the doors. They made sure we were in the house as soon as the streetlights came on. I thought that was pushing it to the edge, but hey! I had to be obedient to them, it was their house and they were in charge.

The Lifestyle

Fashion was (and still is) more highly regarded than education. If you did not have Nike, or Air Jordan, everyone degraded your self-esteem. Many of the kids lived in broken homes. However, this did not stop them from buying expensive clothes. It amazed me to see those kids wearing expensive clothes while their parents could not afford to pay their monthly bills. They complained about being poor but wore clothes that cost more than they could afford. But as for me, my situation was different.

God always provided for us. I cannot remember a day when we did not have something to eat or somewhere to live. My parents worked hard to support us. They are the hardest working people on the face of the earth.

He Saved Me

When I was a baby, the enemy tried to take my life several times. First, when I was a few months old, I had a navel infection that caused excruciating pain. The doctors could not pinpoint the cause of the pain. Miraculously, God supernaturally healed me. I would have died of agony if God did not heal me.

Another time was when I was about three years old; a car ran over me almost killing me. I had to be rushed to the emergency room. Miraculously again, I only had minor injuries. It was only by the grace of God that I did not die. These are just two instances. Because of God's grace and mercy, I was saved to write this book.

Working Together

I thank God for my parents and my grandmother because without their constant help—spiritually, emotionally, and physically—I would not have as much desire to serve God as I do now.

Growing up, I never heard my parents fighting, somehow they were able to work things out privately. My dad went to college in Missouri and then to NJIT to get his Master's Degree in engineering. Unfortunately, he could not get a job as an engineer but ended up working as a carpet cleaner.

While my mom was taking care of us, my dad was out cleaning carpets. We all helped him whenever we could. I remember going to people's houses and saying, "WOW! I want to own a house like this when I grow up." With the little money he made, he made sure that all of our basic needs were met. I never lacked anything because of financial difficulties.

New Clothes

Most of our shopping was done in thrift stores. We could not afford expensive clothes. Other kids made fun of me at times because I did not wear brand name clothes or shoes. That hurt me badly. Unfortunately, that was all I could afford. I stayed away from the park for quite some time of some kid's mockery.

It is a Miracle!

Not long after the ridiculing of my clothes, a miracle happened. God blessed me with money. I took that money and made sure to spend it wisely.

I went to a shoe store and bought my first expensive pair of sneakers, Jason Kidd's. The sneakers cost fifty dollars. I went to another store and bought a silver necklace (which faded after one week), red pants (Swishes brand), and a red Chicago Bulls shirt.

The day, I felt like a movie star. I took my car (which was really my bicycle), washed and wiped it, put on my new outfit and off I went.

While cruising, I made sure not venture into bad neighborhoods. I made sure that everyone saw me, especially those that laughed at me before. That was a memorable day.

Back to Reality

Unfortunately, it did not last too long. After a couple of weeks, my silver necklace had completely lost its color; it looked brownish, reddish, and bluish mixed with something else. My Chicago Bulls shirt was peeling off, and my swishes pants were falling apart. The only thing remaining was my sneakers.

The few dollars I was getting for myself I saved, hoping to help my parents. I hated the conditions my family lived in. I wanted to help my parents badly. However, I could not help them. I did not want my parents to give me anything because I wanted to help them. I remember the nights I prayed and cried, asking God, "Why does this have to happen to my family?"

Sometimes, I heard my parents praying and hoping for more jobs to do so that we could have money to pay the rent and take care of other household necessities. That broke my heart because I could not help them. Several times, I locked myself in the bathroom and cried because of our situation.

Extra cash

As a kid, we played a basketball game called H.O.R.S.E. for quarters. In order to win this game, you had to be the last one standing. We selected at random who went first, second, and so on. After selecting the order, we started the game.

The way this worked is that only shots from the three-point line counted. There were about five or more people involved per game. If someone shot the ball and makes it and the person after him missed it, he received a letter H, and then O, R, and so on. When that happened, it meant he was out of that game and had to wait until the next game.

One day, while getting ready to play horse, I did not have any money. I quickly rushed home and searched until I was able to find a quarter. I rushed back to the park as quickly as I could. Luckily, I arrived just in time before the game started. That day, I went to the park with a quarter and went home with almost five dollars. I felt like a millionaire.

Family

I have the best family in the world. They have always been there to love, encourage, and support me. God blessed me with a wonderful family. Let me tell a little bit about my family.

My parents came from Africa with nothing but a dream that one day their children would not go through the hardships they went through. I remember my mom and dad telling us how hard it was for them growing up in West Africa (Cameroon), a place where there seemed to be no hope for a better future.

However, they did not give up because they had faith in God to "give them a future and hope." God surprised both of them when He opened up the door for them to come to America. It was tough but they kept their faith in God and He provided everything they needed.

Constance, my oldest sister, took such good care of us when we were babies. One of the things I learned from her is to love people in spite of what they have done to you.

She gave up so much for others and us. Because of her faithfulness to God and to people, God blessed her with a wonderful husband.

Antoinette is the next oldest. She too is also a sweetheart. She has always been there for me whenever I needed anything. There were times that I did not have money to take to school and she gave me some. She is also a prayer warrior. Whenever she prays, God moves mightily. God also blessed her with a wonderful husband.

Dominic is my older brother. Growing up, he was the one who gave me the most trouble. We constantly fought and argued over little things.

People knew him as the "hard head" kid who did everything his way. He has always been very protective of me. That helped me because when people found out he was my brother, they immediately stopped messing with me. He recently graduated college with his B.S. in math. He is currently working on his masters. He plans to pursue his PhD as well.

Fidelis Jr. is the newest addition to the Tamin family. He was born in 1999. It is amazing to see what God has done in his life at such an early age. When he was four years old, he had a dream about somebody hurting Antoinette. He woke my parents in the middle of the night, called Antoinette, and told her his dream.

A few days later, Constance called and told my mom she had a similar dream. Because of the revelation, we were able to pray against the attacks of the enemy.

We love him and are proud of him. He brings joy and energy to my family. I cannot wait to see what God has in store for him in the days to come. As for Mathew, keep reading to find out.

My family is important to me. Everyday, I thank God that I am fortunate to be blessed with a family that is there for me whenever I need them.

Chapter 2

A Blessing in the sky

This chapter is dedicated to all the teachers that help change the lives of their students—especially my history teacher Mr. B and my science teacher Ms. Brooks. In the following pages, I will be sharing with you about some of my high school teachers that made an impact in my life. I can never thank them enough.

A word of Hope and Encouragement

Be kindly affectionate to one another with brotherly love, in honor giving preference to one another (Rom. 12:10).

Hanging with the big dawgs

I started high school a few months after turning twelve years old. I was the youngest in my class. I was horrified because I was not as big or tall as the other kids were. I was quiet, shy, and always alone. I spoke only when I was asked a question. I was the last person to walk up to people and start a conversation. In fact, there were times I walked away from conversations.

Academically, I did as well and even better than many students did. However, spiritually I was drowning. I went to church four times a week. I read my Bible only in Sunday school. Sadly, there were times I forgot I had a Bible.

In the midst of everything, I was still a devout church member. I sang in the church choir and played the drums. I went on church trips and participated in every event at the church.

One of the challenges I faced was maintaining my virginity. I was one of the handfuls of kids who were still virgins. Despite my surroundings, I made up my mind not to succumb to having sex or losing my virginity until marriage.

"You're not smart enough"

When I started high school, I knew I needed to take the SAT as a prerequisite to go to college. I did not like taking standardized tests because I did not usually do well in them. After taking the SAT, I did not do well on the math section. I took it again but my math score did not improve.

During my senior year, I had a talk with my guidance counselor about some of the colleges I was interested in going to. I was terrified of talking to her because she was mean, disrespectful, and did not show any enthusiasm for her job.

One day, I finally went to go and see her. We talked about different colleges for me to consider. I told her the specific college I was interested in; she looked at me and said, "You are not smart enough to go there." Those words pierced deep down into my soul. I could not believe that the person that was supposed to help and encourage me was instead discouraging and hurting me.

I did not know what to do so I applied to the university anyway. A few weeks went by as I anxiously waited for the university's response. I finally received it; I was excited to open the letter. When I did open the letter, it said, "Congratulations, you have been accepted!" I was thankful and praised God.

My first semester in college, I had a 4.0 GPA (to God be all the Glory). I went back to my high school to show my counselor how well I did. I was informed that she did not work there anymore (she was fired).

People are not always going to support you in everything you do. Sometimes, you have to be a lone ranger for a while until others get aboard. It was only by the grace of God that I was able to stay encouraged and positive. What a mighty God we serve!

They helped me

My high school did not have the resources others high schools had. We had about eight hundred students. My senior class had about three hundred students and less than half of the class graduated.

Most of the textbooks were not in the best condition. Some were missing pages, while others were severely torn. Some teachers did not care. One teacher told us, "I don't care if you learn or not; as long as I get my check every two weeks I am fine." The only thing my high school was good at was sports, mainly basketball and football. Our basketball team was state champion in 1994. In the school gymnasium, plastered on the walls are banners of all the basketball awards won. Besides sports, some teachers took their job seriously and I commend them for it.

"Write that down somewhere"

Mr. Bryant (a.k.a. Mr. B) was my history teacher; he was the funniest teacher in the school. All the students loved his class because we not only learned but also had fun while learning. One of his favorite statements was, "Write that down somewhere". He always encouraged us to go after our dream regardless of what life brings our way. I had his class during first period, which was good because it set a good mood for the rest of my day.

One morning, I went to school earlier than I usually did. When I arrived, I heard someone saying, "Did you hear that Mr. Bryant is dead?" I rushed quickly to where the statement was coming from to get more information. They continued to say that he had been pronounced dead that morning. I could not believe it!

However, we found out during homeroom that Mr. B did die that morning. That day, everyone was sorrowful and in tears.

I knew he was Muslim and I regret not sharing my faith with him. Writing about this makes me sad. He encouraged and changed my life; he believed in me. He was always there for his students.

You can do math

Ms. Clark was my math teacher who made sure that I did the entire math problem correctly. Math was not my cup of tea. I hated it with a passion, until I had her class.

I thought math involved only numbers. However, to my surprise, I saw x, y, w, and sometimes thought the teacher had a spelling problem. I sat in class trying to figure out these names; suddenly, I realized that I was in a math class not a spelling bee.

Whenever I did not understand a problem, she was always there to help me. I would not have graduated high school if it were not for her. I commend and appreciate her for helping me get through it.

Tough teacher

Ms. Jenkins was my English teacher and also known as the mother of the school. She was firm, tough, and very loving as well. She made sure that I was heading the right direction. Her class was always in order. She was not afraid to wrestle anyone (even the football players). I saw her arm wrestling students to class. Because of the way she treated her students, most of the students loved and respected her.

She listened to me

Ms. Wallace (the history teacher who replaced Mr. Bryan) was a new teacher, fresh out of college, young and beautiful. I have to admit, I had a crush on her. She was caring and a great listener as well. There were times I purposely messed up on my homework or test so that she could have me come and see her after school. I did that because I did not have anyone to talk to.

Whenever I went to go and see her after school, she always asked about what was going on in my life. That meant everything to me because I did not have anyone to listen to me. After talking to her, I felt encouraged, energetic, and much better.

My home girl

Ms. Brooks (a.k.a. Brooksie) was my science teacher. She was a "cool" teacher. Most of the times in her class, we talked about everything else but science. I sometimes wonder if that was a science class or recess.

She too made sure that I was doing well. Brooksie and I had a very special relationship. We understood each other. I appreciated that because she was always there for me.

Unfortunately, Brooksie passed away. When I found out about her death, I was heart broken. She was a heavy smoker. I remember telling her to quit and she kept saying later. She never did. She died of lung cancer.

All these teachers have a special place in my heart, even those that are gone. God put these people in my path because He knew I needed them in order to get to graduate to my next level in life.

RIP Brooksie and Mr. B. Your legacy in my life will never be forgotten. Thank you!

Chapter 3

Order my steps in Your Word

The word of God is a great way of knowing the will and the heart of God. When the word of God is your primary source of direction, you will never get lost.

A word of Hope and encouragement

Trust in the LORD with all your heart, and lean not on your own understanding; in all your ways acknowledge Him, and he shall direct your paths. (Prov. 3:5-6)

Hanging Strong

Whenever I played Horse, I was determined to win. I did everything I had to do to get prepared. I did not let anything or anyone break my focus.

One of the strongest weapons against the enemy is a *made up mind*. He hates those who have their mind made up to serve God. If you want to have a successful relationship with Jesus Christ, this is one of the prerequisites.

In Matthew 13:18, Jesus told His disciples about the parable of a sower:

"The same day went Jesus out of the house, and sat by the sea side. And great multitudes were gathered together unto him, so that he went into a ship, and sat; and the whole multitude stood on the shore. And he spoke many things unto them in parables, saying, Behold, a sower went forth to sow; and when he sowed, some seeds fell by the way side, and the fowls came and devoured them up: Some fell upon stony places, where they had not much earth: and forthwith they sprung up, because they had no deepness of earth: And when the sun was up, they were scorched; and because they had no root, they withered away. And some fell among thorns; and the thorns sprung up, and choked them: But other fell into good ground and brought forth fruit, some a hundredfold, some sixty-fold, some thirty-fold."

In this story, Jesus mentions four different places the seeds fell. "Some fell along the path" (v. 4), "some fell on rocky places" (v.5), "other seeds fell among thorns" (v.7), and "still other seeds fell on good soil" (v.8).

1. Seeds that fell on the path

"When anyone hears the message about the kingdom and does not **understand** it, the evil one comes and snatches away what was sown in his heart. This is the seed sown along the path." (v. 19, emphasis added)

It is important that when we hear the word of God, we make sure that we also understand it. If we don't understand it, not only are we not going to be able to apply it in our lives, but the evil one (Satan) will come and *snatch* away what was sown in our hearts.

James warned us about this. "But be doers of the word, and not hearers only, deceiving yourselves. For if anyone is a hearer of the word and not a doer, he is like a man observing his natural face in a mirror; for he observes himself, goes away, and immediately forgets what kind of man he was. But he who looks into the perfect law of liberty and continues in it, and is not a forgetful hearer but a doer of the work, this one will be blessed in what he does (James 1:22-23, emphasis added).

God wants us to learn how to apply His words in our lives because it draws us closer to Him.

I encourage you to start applying God's word in your life daily. When you read your Bible ask yourself, "How can I apply this in my life?" If you do not understand it, ask the Holy Spirit to give you understanding. You can also ask someone knowledgeable about the Bible like your pastor or youth pastor. Apply it and watch it change you for the better.

2. Seeds that fell on rocky places

"The one who received the seed that fell on rocky places is the man who hears the word and at once receives it with joy. *But since he has no root*, he lasts only a short time. When trouble or persecution comes because of the word, *he quickly* falls away" (v.20, 21, emphasis added).

If you do not stand for something, you will fall for anything. A firm foundation is crucial as a disciple of Christ especially in today's world. A firm foundation helps you through those times when you doubt your faith. If you do not have a solid relationship with Jesus Christ, you are going to believe whatever people tell you.

Persecution, trials, tribulations, and temptations are some of the ways that will test how grounded you are in your faith. The Christian walk seems sweet until you get to that point. Nevertheless, as we say in the hood, "don't be scured."

"My brethren, count it all joy when you fall into various trials, knowing that the testing of your faith produces patience. But let patience have its perfect work, that you may be perfect and complete, lacking nothing" (James 1:2-4). Trials and tribulation will test your loyalty to Jesus Christ.

3. Seeds that fell among thorns

"The one who received the seed that fell among the thorns is the man who hears the word, but the *worries* of this life and the deceitfulness of wealth choke it, making it *unfruitful*." (v. 22, emphasis added).

I use to worry about everything—school, finance, girls. Sometimes when you look at your circumstances, you cannot help but worry. You worry about how you will pay your bills, what you are going to eat, how your college education is going to be paid, and so many other things. When you worry too much about everything, you become "unfruitful." Learn how to entrust God with all your worries.

In Matthew 11:28-30, Jesus encouraged us to, "Come to Me, all you who labor and are heavy laden, and I will give you rest. Take My yoke upon you and learn from Me, for I am gentle and lowly in heart, and you will find rest for your souls. For My yoke is easy and My burden is light." Jesus affirms our safety in Him. "These things I have spoken to you, that in Me you may have peace. In the world you will have tribulation; but be of good cheer, **I have overcome the world**" (John 16:33, emphasis added). It feels good to know that I do not have to worry anymore about anything. Do not pray and then worry.

4. Seeds That Fell on Good Soil

"But the one who received the seed that fell on good soil is the man who hears the word and *understands it*. He *produces* a crop, yielding a hundred, sixty or thirty times what was sown" (v. 23, emphasis added).

These are the types of seeds that God wants His children to be—fruitful and productive. The people that produce fruits are the ones who did not let the enemy snatch the word of God away from their heart. After reading God's word, they applied it in their everyday life and grew. They stood firm throughout the trials, tribulations, temptations, and persecutions.

In spite of the drama in their lives, they trusted God and never gave up. When they could not see how their bills were going to be paid, they did not worry or doubt because they knew, "My God shall **supply all your** need according to His riches in glory by Christ Jesus" (Phil. 4:19, emphasis added).

A woman was asked about the secret of winning the spiritual battle. Her reply was, "When the devil knocks, I let Jesus answer."

Whenever it feels like your world is crashing down on you, call on Jesus, and He will be there for you. "For He Himself has said, I will never leave you nor forsake you." (Heb. 13:5) Without His help, we cannot do anything on our own. Remember, when Satan knocks at your door, get Jesus to answer.

Chapter 4

Heartbreak hotel

Rejection and heartbreaks can be very challenging to deal with. Unfortunately, most of us cannot escape it. Most of us have to go through it in order to become the person God created us to be. I too, have had several heartaches and disappointment. I heard someone once say, "Rejection is God's protection": what a profound but yet accurate statement.

A word of Hope and Encouragement

Come to Me, all you who labor and are heavy laden, and I will give you rest. Take My yoke upon you and learn from Me, for I am gentle and lowly in heart, and you will find rest for your souls. For My yoke is easy and My burden is light. (Matt. 11:28-30)

She didn't know my name

It was until high school that I started noticing the female species. Before that, I did not want anything to do with them. I thought they were the grossest creatures on the face of the earth. I never wanted to sit next to girls or even talk to them. However, things changed.

One day in gym class, I noticed this beautiful girl—Michelle. I wanted to talk to her but I was too shy to say anything. Every day I came to class, I looked at her but did not utter a word to her. I came up with several dumb ways for her to notice me but it did not work. However, all of this was about to change.

As the fourth marking period went by, I figured this would be a perfect time for me to make my move. Therefore, I came up with a plan to get this girl to notice me.

On the last day of school before our winter break, I skipped class to go to her lunch period. The day before, I had gone to the store and bought her a Christmas card.

I asked Wes, a good friend of mine, to do me a favor. I gave him the card to give to Michelle and told him where I would be standing if she wanted to know whom the card came from. After he gave her the card, she asked, "Who is it from?"

"Mathew,"

"Who is Mathew?" she asked. When Wes pointed to where I was supposed to be standing, I had disappeared. I was nervous and shy. I ran upstairs as fast as I could.

While in class, I could not help but wonder what her response was. I sat there nervously waiting for that period to end so that I could find out what she said. As soon as the bell rang, I ran out of class to look for Wes. When he saw me, he had the look on his face that said, "You are a punk." I asked him what happened. He said he gave her the letter but she

22

did not know whom it was from and when he pointed to where I was suppose to be standing, I had mysteriously disappeared.

During the winter break, I could not wait to start school so that I could see Michelle. The last night of the winter break, I tossed and turned, thinking about Michelle.

The following morning, I woke up early and ran to school. When I arrived at school, all the students were standing outside because gang members tried to burn down the school. I did not care about that; all I wanted to do was to find Michelle (even though she did not know me) and just look at her.

We were allowed back in school after a couple of days with the offices in bad shape. As I sat in class that day, something amazing happened. She walked up to me and said, "Mathew"? I turned around and looked, it was Michelle. I could not believe it. I started shaking and sweating. I did not know what she was going to say or do to me.

"Is your name Mathew?"

"Yes"

"So you are the one who sent me the Christmas card?"

I am in big trouble. Maybe it was not a good idea to give her the card. Maybe I should not have said anything, or maybe I should have given it to her myself, I said to myself.

"Yeah," I replied.

"Why didn't you give it to me yourself?"

"I was shy."

After talking to her for a couple of minutes, I was not as nervous as I was before. I later found out she thought I was cute and very nice. Unfortunately, things did not work out. I have not heard from her since then.

"I don't like you like that"

Her name was Kory; she was a cheerleader, about 5'5". She was in my history class. The more I saw her in class, the more I fell in "lust," thinking it was love, with her. I was becoming bolder and more confident when approaching girls. I thought Kory was cute and I wanted to get to know her.

As the days went by, I worked on a plan to accomplish this difficult mission ahead of me. After several days of working on this "great" plan, I was exhausted.

The day finally came when I was to unleash my "master" plan. I asked another friend of mine to do me a favor. I used the same procedure as before. I told him to give her the letter and if she asked who it was to tell her. This time however, I ran before he gave her the letter. She read the letter but did not know whom I was. After a couple of days, someone told her who I was.

It was valentine season and I was going to ask her to be my valentine. I was praying and hoping she would say yes.

A few days before Valentine's Day, I walked to her locker with confidence, putting my shyness aside, and said, "Hi Kory, how are you doing?"

"I am doing fine."

In my mind, that was a great start. From the looks of it, I was confident everything was going to work out as planned.

"Can I ask you a question?"

"Sure."

"Will you be my valentine?"

She paused, looked me and said, "I don't like you like that." When she said that, I felt as if someone stabbed my heart. I did not know what to do or say. I slowly walked away with my head down and tears in my eyes.

The sad part about this was that many people knew about it. For months, I cried myself to sleep every night. I felt the reason why she did not like me was that I was ugly. Because of that incident, I became depressed for a while. I felt no girl would ever want to go out with an ugly person like myself. I lost my self-esteem, self-confidence, and self-motivation.

Come on let's dance

The Sadie Hawkins dance was a time when students had the opportunity to have fun. It was our annual homecoming party held in the cafeteria. Everyone was looking forward to it. When I heard about it, I was excited to go. This meant going out with a date (something new to me). After being disappointed about being dateless, I decided to go anyway.

The day of the dance, I went in my closet and picked out an outfit for the party. I did not have a ride so I walked. It was about a twenty-five minute walk. By the time I arrived at the school, I was tired.

While waiting for the party to start, I watched as a limousine, a Mercedes Benz, and other luxury cars dropped people off. For a moment, it seemed like it was a prom. There I was with my Al Capone suite standing by the door watching and smiling at people as they came in with their dates.

As everyone danced, I sat with others who were also dateless (about a handful of us). I was sad because I wanted someone to dance with me. I was not the type of person to get up and start dancing with anybody. I was too shy to do that. I was afraid the girl might not want to dance with me and shove me away.

After a couple of hours, the DJ announced the last song; "Love you like I did" by 112. (At the time, the song was just released and I loved it). The lights were dim as people dance. I looked and saw Kory dancing with her date. That hurt me because I wished that could have been me. As I watched others dance, a girl came to me and said, "You don't have a date, do you?"

"No, I don't."

"Would you like to dance?"

"Sure." I thought that was sweet of her.

I stood with up and started dancing. I was excited and honored that she asked to dance with me. After taking a few steps, she said, "you don't know how to slow dance, do you?"

"No, I don't."

This was my first time slow dancing and I did not know what to do. She asked someone else to dance with me because of that. As I danced with this other girl, I heard, "Ouch."

"What's wrong?" I asked.

"You are stepping on my feet."

With tears in my eyes, I said, "You don't have to dance with me if you don't want to, it's okay. You can sit down. Thank you though."

She left before I complete my sentence. That is when I realized, "Houston, we've got a problem." Sadly, all of this happened during the first verse of the song.

I left the dance floor, went to the bathroom, and cried. I walked back to the cafeteria sat down and acted as if nothing happened. That night when I went home, I cried all night. I felt embarrassed, unloved, uncared for, and unwanted.

Chapter 5

I almost let go

In life, there are certain times that some of us wish we were never born, primarily because of certain situations. However, it is in times like these that we truly find out how important our relationship with God is. If you are going through a difficult time, do not give up. I know it is easier said than done. If I did not give up, I know that you will not either. You have come too far to start over.

A word of Hope and Encouragement

For in the time of trouble He shall hide me in His pavilion; In the secret places of His tabernacle He shall hide me; He shall set me high upon a rock. (Ps. 37:5)

He kept me

In spite of my surroundings, God kept me and He can do the same for you. If you are in a situation where everything seems to be contrary to your faith, I encourage you to hold on to God. He will never let you down.

It will get difficult sometimes, but do not give up. God has not brought you this far to let you go. I love what the songwriter says:

"I just can't give up now

I've come too far from where I started from

Nobody told me the road would be easy

And I don't believe He's brought me this far, to leave me."

The Christian road is not easy. If anyone told you that it is, that is not true. Jesus went through difficult times. Sometimes God allows us to go through certain things to make us stronger as well as to encourage others.

Several times, I cried myself to sleep. I wondered why God allow certain things to happen to me. Why this, why that. However, instead of asking why God allowed you to go through something, move on. If you keep thinking unpleasant thoughts about the past, it can destroy your present, and dictate your future.

God is not looking for crybabies, people that complain and nag about everything. Sometimes God allows certain things to happen to us so that He can teach us valuable lessons. Another reason He does that is so that we can be able to stand against Satan and not surrender.

I thank God that I grew up in the environment I did. I thank God that I bought clothes for one dollar. I thank God for letting me experience some of the things I experienced. Complaints will never get you anywhere in life. Sometimes, things happen to us that are not fair, but life is not fair. You cannot cry every time something does not go your way. Because of my upbringing, I have learned to, "**Bless** the Lord at **all** times and His praise shall continually be in my mouth" (Ps. 34:1, emphasis added).

If you can bless God when you are poor, you will not have any problems blessing Him when you have money. If you can bless God when you are hurting, you will not have any problems blessing Him when He mends your broken heart. When you learn to bless God in the midst of your storm, you can also bless Him through the joy. God will not let Satan defeat you. He wants you to be victorious always.

The Bible reminds us to, "Count it all joy when you face trials and tribulations" (James 1:2). If we do not go through hard time in life, we will not learn how to appreciate what we have.

God is looking for people like David to face Goliath without fear. People that will march into the enemy's camp and take back everything he has stolen from them, their family, and friends.

Now is not the time to sit back and regret all the mistakes you made in the past. Step into the promise God made to you. It is time to fight, not to cry. Remember, "You are a **chosen generation**, a **royal priesthood**, a **holy nation**, His own special people, that you may proclaim the praises of Him who called you out of darkness into His marvelous light"(1 Pet. 2:9, emphasis added). Step into your rightful position as kings and queens. Do not give up! You have come too far to start over.

I almost gave it away

I once had a "close call." I never thought I would find myself in such a compromising situation.

One afternoon at a friend's house, I saw this girl and thought she was attractive. I wanted to talk to her but I did not know what to say. I was shy and afraid to talk to girls.

The following day, I saw this girl hanging out with a close friend of mine. I could not believe my friends knew her and did not tell me. I told my friend to go tell her that I like her and wanted to talk to her. The plan was for her to meet me inside his room.

I went into his room and waited for her. While waiting, I became extremely nervous. I did not know what to expect. Moreover, this was going to be my first time getting close to a girl. My friend told me that whatever I was going to do to it fast because his dad would be home soon.

About five minutes later, I heard a knock on the door. I did not know if I should open it or run. After calming down, I said, "Come in." When the door opened up, I saw this young hot girl coming towards me. I knew I was about to have a heavenly experience. I sat on the bed waiting to see what she would do. This was my first time meeting the girl.

She walked in and said, "Hi." I did not know if I should say, "Hi," or "bring it on baby." I looked at her and said something. After our brief introduction, she sat next to me. I thought, "Man, I just won the jackpot."

I felt as if I was in a boxing match waiting for my opponent to get ready. Even though this was not a boxing match, it was going to be very intense and I did not plan to lose this one for the world. The look she gave me translated as, "Come on and kiss me." I was afraid because I had never kissed a girl before and this was going to be my first time. I thought about it for a few minutes and decided, "What do I have to lose." I put my arm around her and started kissing her.

As we kissed, and things started getting hot. I felt the room's temperature rise one hundred degrees. All of a sudden, I heard my friend made a sound (giving me a cue that his dad was home). I did not know what to do. If I had wings, it would have been the perfect time to use them. When we heard his father's voice, we both rushed out the back door like superman chasing superwoman.

I had fun kissing the girl. It felt great! I was angry his dad had to show up at that crucial time when everything seemed to be going my way. However, that did not discourage me; I was determined to complete the work I had started. I invited her to come back another day so that we could finish what we started.

A few days later, she came back. This time, we went to a different location.

I was excited and could not wait to get started. I sat on the bed waiting for her come to me. It worked. We both stared each other in the eyes for a couple of minutes. This was strange because we had been in a similar situation before and everything went well. I thought to myself, "Man, I hope we don't do this all day."

After staring at each other without saying anything for about a couple of minutes, she started getting closer to me. Everything was going great. I was having a great time.

I was still a "Christian". However, Jesus was not on my mind at the time. I was not thinking about Him at all. The only thing on my mind was that girl.

Something in me did not feel right. Unfortunately, I could not put my finger on it. I felt bad. I fought the feeling and tried to ignore it but it did not work.

No one told me what to do in a compromising situation. All I was taught was to "preach the gospel; praise God, and everything else will be alright."

The make out session was starting to get more intense than it did before. I wanted to try some of what I saw on TV. However, I was "scured" to do that because I did not know what her reaction would be. Would she allow me or slap me. Well, there was only one way to find out.

I decided I was going to try to touch her sexually because after kissing for a while, I was bored and wanted to try something new and exciting.

Something amazing happened when I tried to make my move. For some odd reason, I could not get my hands to touch her as planned. I tried but I felt like someone kept pushing my hands away. If God did not intervene that day, I would have lost my virginity. It was a matter of when, not if. Nevertheless, for some miraculous reason, I froze and I did not understand why.

After trying and not getting anywhere, I decided to let this girl go home. After incident, I had mixed emotions about what had happened. I felt convicted and confused.

I surrender all

Like most kids, I wanted to get involved in a relationship. I tried having a girlfriend, but I was not able to get one. I could not understand why whenever I tried talking to girls, it never worked out for me, but it did for everyone else. One thing or another happened. I did not appreciate men taking advantage of women. All I wanted was to have a girlfriend.

Because of not being able to have a girlfriend, I was depressed. I felt the reason why I could not get a girl was that I was ugly. I thought of myself as one of the ugliest people in the world and imagined that was why I could not get a girl. I felt unloved and wanted to find someone who would love me for me.

At the time, I did not understand God's love. Other people's acceptance meant more to me than God's love and acceptance. I did not give God enough time to heal my broken heart. Instead, I looked for people to fill the void. I lost my focus on God because of that. The Internet became my best friend. I spent hours on matchmaker sites, looking for love. Some of the conversations I had with those girls on and offline was not Christ oriented. I became hooked. My relationship with God deteriorated because of that.

I always cautioned people about going to "matchmaker" sites because you might go there just to find a "friend" but instead you get more involved in it than you originally planned to. That is how I started. I was only looking for "friends." I was not reading my Bible or praying. I choose girls over God.

Maybe you are like that, you try to get involved with every person you find attractive, or you have to be with someone in order to be "cool." You think that you are not attractive just because you do not have a girlfriend or a boyfriend. That is not true. You are fine the way God made you. God did not make a mistake when He created you.

I thank God that things happened the way they did. If it had had happen any other way, I would have been more hurt. If God did not break up my friendship with certain girls, I would have lost my virginity. Though it was painful, it built me up. Because of the pain and drama, I had to stop doing what I was and get right with God. "What doesn't kill you only makes you stronger." That is exactly what happened to me. When you keep God first, everything else always works out.

Do not be in such a hurry to get into relationships. Do not date because everyone else is dating. Let God keep developing you into the person He wants you to be. Do not let peer pressure dictate how you live. Avoid it as best as you can. Pray and ask God to help you stay focused. He did it for me and He can do it for you.

Pray and ask God to give you the strength to stay pure and holy until He sends you your future mate. One of my prayers during this time was "keep me Lord." In other words, in the midst of all the sexual temptation I faced and had to deal with, I asked God to put a hedge of protection around me so that I would stay pure and holy for Him and my future wife. If you have messed up, it is not too late to ask God to cleanse you and keep you.

Young Men

As young men, we have to learn how to respect young women. We should not look at them as objects, but rather as beautiful creations handmade by Our Creator. We have to learn how to treat them right, and love every day.

We should not put our hands where they do not belong. Their bodies are not where you learn your geographic locations. As men of God, we have no right to explore their bodies. When you respect women, God will bless you with a beautiful girl. He wants to bless you with someone special.

Young Ladies

As a young woman, do not lower your standard even when it seems like the person you have always prayed for seems to be out of sight. God knows the desire of your heart and He will give it to you.

It bothers me to see beautiful young women selling themselves to people for money, attention, or cars. All of those things are only temporary. Your body is a temple of the living God. That is why the Bible encourages us to take care of it. One of the most common cliché men use is "If you love me you will have sex with me"—which is not true. The translation of that in modern terms is, "if you love me, you will give me the most precious gifts God has given to you to share with the right person."

If a person loves you, he would want to protect your virginity rather than take it away from you. If a person loves and respects you, he will not touch you in a sexual way. Rather, he will refrain from it.

That is why it is important to find a God-fearing man; a man who will not succumb to that temptation but instead cherish you as the princess God created you to be; a man who will see you as a mighty woman of valor, not a sex object. As hard as it seems, there are men like that, waiting for their princess-you.

God has that special person for you to marry. He is on his way to sweep you off your feet. God is preparing you so that He can send your knight in shining armor. Do not let anyone tell you that you are not beautiful. Always remember that you are the apple of God's eyes. Let Him continue to work in you. Do not rush to look for that person, but pray that God would send him to you.

If you are serious about letting God choose your partner for you, I encourage you to read, "When God writes your love story" by Eric and Leslie Ludy. It is a great book.

"No good thing will He withhold from those who walk upright" (Ps. 84:11). When you walk upright, God will see to it that you get what you deserve.

Chapter 6

God's will is what I want

Things can be extremely challenging when you are not in the will of God. Sometimes, God has to take us through certain situations in order to get in His will. As you read this, keep in mind one important fact about God's will. The Will of God will never take you where the Grace of God cannot keep you.

A word of Hope and Encouragement

My sheep hear My voice, and I know them, and they follow Me. And I give them eternal life, and they shall never perish; neither shall anyone snatch them out of My hand. My Father, who has given them to Me, is greater than all; and no one is able to snatch them out of My Father's hand. (John 10:27-29)

Things changed

It was my homecoming football game my senior year and the most anticipated game of the year. Our opponent was the best in our conference. Weeks before the game, our coaches made sure that we practiced as needed in order to get ready for the big game.

The day before the game, we had light practice so that no one would get hurt and not be able to play the following day. That week, we were given the royal treatment, even the teachers treated us like kings. (Man, did I cherish those days). When the day finally came, everyone was excited and could not wait to start the game.

However, less than ten minutes in the game our team was down by two touchdowns (14 points). We tied the game in the first few minuets of the third quarter.

With ten seconds left in the game, my coach told me to get ready to kick the field goal (hopefully the winning one). As I ran out on the field, I looked at the crowd and saw hundreds of people watching and cheering for us to win. When I looked at the distance I had to kick the ball, it seems like a thousand yards. Even though I had made this in practice the day before, I was not sure if I was going to be able to it again. The pressure and nervousness scared me.

I walked on the field as the referee blew the whistle for us to get ready. I took three short steps back and three to the left. I heard "ready, hut… hut." When I looked on the sideline and the bleachers, some people had their hands crossed, while others had their heads down. The nervousness became worse. Our entire season was on the line. My team depended on me as well as my school.

When the holder finally caught the ball, I noticed it was wobbling. I could not stop and say, "Slow down everyone, let's fix the ball from wobbling so that I can get a better kick." Therefore, I decided to kick the ball anyway.

When I kicked it, I saw it going straight down the middle and I knew it was going to make it all the way to the end zone. After kicking the ball, two humungous linebackers with a combined weight of 550 pounds knocked me down. For a second, I was not sure what happened. I stood up and started walking out of the field. Sadly, the ball did not make it to the end zone. I was sad and disappointed for letting everyone down.

New Direction

Growing up, I loved playing sports—basketball, soccer, tennis, and football. I wanted to be the next Michael Jordan (along with every other kid in America). I worked hard at every sport I played with the hopes of becoming a professional player. Maybe that sounds like you. You think you have everything planned and know exactly where to go and what to do.

However, for me, God had a different plan in mind for my life. He did not want me to become the next Michael Jordan or pro athlete (not to say that He will do the same for you). He wanted me to share His gospel to the lost. However, before that game, I was selfish and wanted to do things my way. I was determined to become the next super star athlete. Sports were everything to me. I did everything I needed to do to get me to where I wanted to go. Unfortunately, I found myself getting hurt day by day, making it harder for me to start and finish my football, soccer, or basketball seasons.

After I missed the field goal, I realized that God is in control of everything. It does not matter what you do: if it is not in the will of God, it will not work. It might feel good temporarily, but at some point, you will get tired of it.

I kept on running away from my calling without being aware of it. I spent more time playing sports and watching TV than I did reading my Bible or spending time with God.

The more my athletic skills improved, the more my Bible knowledge decreased. I was drowning without being aware of it.

After remembering that it is only in the will of God that I can succeed, I decided to trade sports for God. I told the Lord, "Where you lead me, I will go." I am not implying that you cannot love sports and God at the time. However, when you put sports or anything instead of God that's when there is a problem. God is a jealous God. The first commandment is, "Thou shall have no other gods besides me", letting us know that in everything we do, God should always be number one.

Meaning of life

One of the biggest questions asked by people of all ages today is "how do I find out my purpose in life"? Everywhere I go, I hear people asking that question.

Before going to college, I knew I wanted to major in psychology. As I went along in my studies, I developed a deeper interest in music as well. Because I was not certain where God was leading me, I kept my options open, taking music and psychology courses.

Here are some important things to keep in mind while on the search for your purpose:

It is not about you

God knew you before anyone else did. In other words, "Before I formed you in the womb I *knew you.* (Jer. 1:5, emphasis added). Before the foundation of this earth and long before your mom and your dad knew each other, God knew you. He had everything mapped out for you. He is waiting for you to come to Him so that He can reveal it to you.

The search for purpose has puzzled people for thousands of years. That is because we do not go to the source. Instead, we begin at the wrong point—ourselves. Instead of asking God about it, we start asking self-centered questions like, what do I want to be? What should I do with my life? What are my goals and dreams for my future? However, by us focusing on ourselves, we will never find out what our purpose on earth is.

In our society today, being successful is important and something we should all strive to become. People tell you when you put your mind to it you can do it. However, being successful and fulfilling your life's purpose is not all the same issue. You could reach all your personal goals and dreams, becoming successful by the world's standard and still miss the purpose for which God created you.

You have to understand that your purpose is far greater than your own fulfillment, your peace of mind, your happiness, or even your future mate. It is greater than your family, career, or even your wildest dreams and ambitions. It is important to understand that you were born by His purpose and for His purpose.

How then do you discover your purpose? You have two options. First, you can **speculate**—most people choose this because they guess and theorize and, besides, it seems easy. You do not have to be a rocket scientist to do this. The second is through **Revelation**—turning to the Word of God for help. Personally, I think this is the easiest way because the Bible gives you clear guidelines and principles.

Remember, "It's in Christ that we find out who we are and what we are living for. Long before we first heard of Christ and got our hopes up, He had his eyes on us, had designs on us for glorious living, part of the overall purpose he is working out in everything and everyone" (Eph. 1:11).

God is awesome! He knew…

- David was going to defeat Goliath and later become the King of Israel before David was born. (See 1 Samuel. 17)

- Moses was going to lead the children of Israel out of Egypt. (see Exodus 13)

- Daniel was going to be thrown in the lion's den. (See Daniel 6)

- Saul was going to become Paul and later write half of the New Testament. (See Acts 9)

- Peter was going to deny Jesus three times before the rooster crowed. (See Mark 14:66-72)

- You were going to be reading this book today.

He planned it before you existed, without your input! You may choose your career, spouse, hobbies, and many other areas of your life, but you do not get to choose your purpose. That is something only God can do.

You are NOT an accident

Some people feel as if their birth was a mistake either because of their parents, close relatives, or because of other people. That is the lie of the enemy. Your birth was not a mistake, an accident, or a coincidence. Your parents may not have planned you, but God did. Your birth did not surprise God. In fact, He was expecting you. Long before your mother conceived you, God already conceived you in His mind. It is not fate, nor chance, nor luck, nor coincidence that you are breathing and alive at this moment. You are alive because God created you. I heard a story that touched me; let me share it with you.

A boy lived alone with his father. The father worked too much, making it difficult to spend time with his son. Whenever this boy needed advice, his dad was never around. He became lonely, filled with anger, pain, and hurt.

One day the police arrested him for committing a crime. "Why did you do it?" asked a reporter. He paused and said, "It's better to be wanted for something than not to be wanted at all."

It bothers me when I talk to people that feel as if they are here by accident. Many people, especially young people, feel as if no one cares. Parents as well as godly men and women should take responsibility in a teenager's life because they will be surprised how much difference they can make.

You are fine just the way you are. Extra makeup does not reveal your true beauty, but only covers it up. Working out for attention does not change who you are. God purposely chose your race, the color of your skin, your hair, and every other feature. He knew what gifts and talents you are going to have. "You know me inside and out, and you know every bone in my body; you know exactly how I was made, bit by bit, how I was sculpted from nothing into something" (See Ps. 139:1-3).

Because God made you for a reason, He also decided when you would be born and how long you would live there. He choose the exact time and place of your birth.

Most amazing, God decide how you would be born. God had a plan in creating you. It does not matter whether your parents were good, bad, or indifferent. God knew your parents were the only two people in the entire world with the DNA He needed to create you. You may not have a good relationship with your parents, but be thankful to God for them. Without them, we would not be here.

Where is your heart? Everyone's life is driven by something, whether positive or negative. What is that thing that you spend most of your time doing? Even though this may not be what your purpose is, it can give you some idea or sense of direction to finding your purpose.

Music

As I mentioned earlier, when I started college, I knew that the Lord was leading me towards psychology. After my first semester, I declared it as my major. During that time, I started taking music classes as well.

While taking elementary piano, it sparked my interest in playing the piano. I felt a strong passion for music that increased daily.

During that time, I was confused about what to do—music or psychology. I knew God was leading me towards psychology, but my passion to play the piano increased everyday. I was caught between playing the piano or studying psychology.

However, as much as I liked music, it took some time for me to see where God was leading me at the time.

Even though you might have a strong desire to do something and be good at it, it may not necessarily be what God want you to do at that point and time. You may have been interested in a particular thing for that season. In my case, God wanted me to learn how to play the piano so that I could write songs.

Maybe you have a gift of singing, writing, or playing a musical instrument. That could be God's way of telling you something. Some people are waiting for God to give them a sign from heaven. Unfortunately, God seldom does that anymore. He has given us His word, and minds to think. This world is in need of anointed singers, musicians, and songwriters.

Look at all the junk that is in the world. God wants to use your gift to impact the lives of others. Do not hide the gift that is inside of you. Allow God to develop it so that in due season, you will be able to minister to thousands or even millions of people.

If you feel God is calling you to the music ministry, take music lessons in order to prepare yourself so that when God opens doors for you to minister, you will be able to walk in it and not doubt.

If you are a songwriter, allow God to give you the words to your lyrics. If you play an instrument, spend time to practice and improve your skills. When you let God develop the gifts already inside of you, with preparation and His timing, your gift will be a blessing to the world. Keep in mind that your gift can only take you as far as your character allows you.

Teaching

Some people love to teach. They always find themselves explaining things. They are always available to answer questions.

This world is in desperate need of godly teachers. I love being around people like these because I learn from them.

If you feel called to teach, spend time reading God's word as well as other books. James 1:5 says, "If any of you lacks wisdom, let him ask of God, who gives to all liberally and without reproach, and it will be given to him." God wants His people to be equipped in ministry.

Youth Ministers

Some people have youth ministry calling written all over them. People with this calling usually have a desire to see young people going the right direction. They feel responsible whenever a teenager messes up. However, many ignore the calling.

I was watching TBN one day and TD Jake's wife was being interviewed. She made a profound statement. She said, "It's going to take the youth to reach the youth." That is true because young people are more prone to listen to someone that is close to their age.

You might be reading this and feel convicted because you know God has called you to be a leader amongst your peers. Do not ignore it, just pray about it.

Politics

Whenever people start talking about politics, an argument is usually waiting to explode. Some argue about which party is better: Democratic, Republican, or, according to Rod Parsley, the "Christ-ocratic party."

During my sophomore year in college, I had the opportunity to go to City and the Hill, a program for youth held by the NJFPC (New Jersey Family Policy Counsel). The program was designed to equip young people who are interested in politics to represent the body of Christ.

When we started debating about certain issues, I noticed that certain Kids were born to be politicians. God is raising a generation that will speak what the Lord says and not be afraid or ashamed of what others will say. This generation of political leaders will address many prominent and pertinent issues such as abortion, pornography, drugs, and homosexuality from a Biblical point of view and not be concerned about the response or reaction from people.

Benefits of knowing your purpose

There is much benefit when you know your purpose. You now know where to go and what to do. Here are some of the benefits:

1. Purpose in life

Without God, life has no purpose, and without purpose, life has no meaning. "For I know the plans I have for you, declares the Lord, plans to prosper you and not to harm you, plans to give you hope and a future". (Jeremiah. 29:11) God is able to do far more than we would ever dare to ask or even dream of definitely beyond our highest prayers, desires, thoughts, and hopes.

It gives you an inner peace that says, "Everything is going to be okay because I have Jesus by my side." If you are not sure of what your purpose in life is, you will be constantly worried and stressed.

However, when you learn to "let go and let God" you will be surprised about what He can do for you, in you, and through you. God does not want you to worry about your future; He will take care of that for you. All He asks of you is to put your faith and trust in Him.

2. Life becomes simple

Your purpose becomes the standard you use to evaluate which activities are essential and which are not. You simply ask, "Does this activity help me fulfill one of God's purposes for my life?"

People who do not know their purpose try to do too much, and that causes stress, fatigue, and conflict. You only have enough time to do God's will.

You will end up doing nothing if you try to do everything. No single individual is called to do everything. If you are doing your will and not His, it will hinder your ministry. I like the saying, "some are called, and some went." This describes many ministers today. They put their time and energy in doing something contrary to their calling.

3. You become more focused

You become effective by being selective. Without a clear purpose, you will keep changing directions, jobs, majors, relationships, churches, or other things, hoping each change will settle the confusion or fill the emptiness in your heart. You think maybe this time it will be different, but it does not solve your real problem —lack of focus and purpose.

It is important to stay focused because if we are not focused on God, we give Satan an opportunity to enter in our lives. As the saying goes, "An idle mind is the devil's workshop." If you do not stay focused on God, you will find yourself in the devil's territory, a terrible place to find yourself. However when you are focused, you know what you are intended to do.

Chapter 7

Be holy, for I am Holy

God wants His children to live holy because He is holy. However, many Christians are not living a holy lifestyle. Many are struggling with sexual sins-lust, masturbation, pornography, and other things. God's love is power in that in spite of what we do, He still loves us. Holiness is a commandment, not an option. When you live holy, God will bless you.

A word of Hope and Encouragement

I beseech you therefore, brethren, by the mercies of God, that you present your bodies as a living sacrifice, holy, acceptable to God, which is your reasonable service. (Rom. 12:1)

The road less traveled

As Christians, we are going to face difficult situations. Some situations require more prayers than others. There will be times when we fall and the enemy is going to make it seem as if we cannot get back up. That is not true. We serve a God of a second chance. He will never leave you nor forsake you. He is always going to be by your side even when things do not seem to be working your way.

When you want to give up, get down on your knees, and talk to your heavenly Father and He will answer you. Do not listen to Satan. All you have to do is call on the name of the Lord. "The name of the LORD is a **strong tower**; the righteous run to it and are safe" (Prov. 18:10, emphasis added).

I started college three months after turning sixteen. Prior to that, there were some things in my life that needed deliverance. One of them was lust.

I had this problem because I watched things that were unhealthy for my spiritual growth. I had too much junk in my head and God wanted to clean it out.

When most high school students, especially graduating seniors, think about college, they think of it as a place of "freedom." They will not have their parents to watch over them or tell them what to do. Because of that, many people change after their first year of college. College is a place of freedom. Your parents or guardians are not monitoring you.

It is vital to have a firm foundation or else people will persuade you to believe that the God you serve is nothing but a figment of your imagination.

One of the things I did before starting college was to make sure that I knew who Jesus is for me so that no one can tell me that He does not exits.

My first year, I became involved with different Christian organizations. During that year, I saw what the college life was all about—girls, parties, girls, and more girls.

The temptation increased for me. I knew that was going to happen because the Lord had told me before going to college. Everywhere I looked, most of the girls were half-dressed.

Back then, I looked at every girl's derrière that walked by. This was new to me because all my life I had been protected by my parents so much that when I was alone, I felt like a bird released from the cage to experience life on its own.

Whenever I looked at girls, I did it in a subtle way, making sure that no one noticed. However, God did. God knew that was going to be one of my weaknesses.

At the time, whenever a young woman walked by who was dressed provocatively, my flesh cued me to get ready to lust. Two thoughts went through my head—to look or not to look. Sadly, ten out of ten times I looked.

There were times when I looked but not as soon as she passed because I knew other people were going to be looking as well. So I waited a few seconds after she passed, then looked. I had to do it that way because I was known on campus as Mr. Holy, Pastor, and Bishop. I did not want to ruin that reputation.

You might be struggling with the battle of the eyes and need some help, do not worry, there is hope. I will show you how you can overcome this with the Blood of the Lamb.

Maybe you do not think there is anything wrong with lusting. If you see an attractive woman walking by, dressed very seductively, looking too much will invoke sexual thoughts in your mind, which is lusting. You will plant that seed and once you do, it takes twice as long to remove that image from your head. I have heard people use different

51

excuses for lusting after women, one of which is: "I am admiring the beautiful creation of God." That is not true. You can admire a young woman's beauty without undressing her with your eyes.

Temptation or being tempted is not a sin. Succumbing to temptation is what makes it a sin. Jesus warned us (men especially) about lusting after women. "But I say to you, that whoever looks at a woman to lust for her had already committed adultery with her in his heart" (Matthew 5:28).

Keeping it real

Masturbating is another issue God delivered me from. I read a Christian article that claimed that ninety-five percent of Christian males and sixty-five percent of Christian females masturbate. With the way our society is going, that number is increasing, due in part to the capability and accessibility of the Internet.

Most churches are ignoring these topics. The world tells you that it is okay to masturbate and watch pornography, when it is not. Your body is a living temple of God, and God cannot dwell in an unclean vessel.

Everyday, young girls get pregnant because of the lack of sexual education in the church. It is time for the church to start educating young people about purity. Abortion and sexually transmitted diseases is proliferating in the church. Some Christians thinks it is fine to have pre-marital sex as long as you love someone, but it is not fine. It saddens my heart to see that most churches are not doing anything about this. Unfortunately, everyone has to answer to God on Judgment day.

There will always be something in our lives not pleasing to God as long as we are in this flesh. The flesh wants to do what the Spirit does not. We all make mistakes. God understands that. There is not a single person in the

Bible (excluding Jesus) who never messed up. David watched another man's wife taking a bath. Peter denied Jesus. Paul crucified Christians. The list goes on.

I am grateful that in spite of the challenges I was around, God kept me. He can keep you too.

Determination

I made a covenant with God while struggling with purity. You can always tell when you are doing something that is not pleasing to God because you feel dirty and guilty. I was going through a reconstruction stage in my spiritual life. God had to do some remolding in me. He took away the old things and replaced them with something new and fresh. "If any man be in Christ, he is a **new creation**. Old things are passing away, behold! All things are new (2 Cor. 5:17, emphasis added).

I was determined to stay pure and holy regardless of the price I had to pay. I was delivered but I was not disciplined enough to maintain my deliverance. It is as important to stay free as it is to become free because, "Where the Spirit of the Lord is, there is liberty" (2 Cor. 3:17).

As I lived holy for God, the enemy attacked me in every area of my life. He wanted to see if I was truly delivered. He tried everything he could to make me fall. However, I was determined to maintain my freedom in Jesus.

I sometimes fell, but after falling, I asked for repentance and moved on. The Holy Spirit gently encouraged me to keep going. He never condemned me.

I once heard a soft voice said to me, "If you will stop doing this and stay close to me, I will take you higher in me." I knew that was the Holy Spirit. Immediately I began to weep. I felt unworthy of God's love. Even though I did things He did not like, going against His word, He still wanted to take me, use me, and love me as if nothing ever happened.

A few days later, I heard the same voice in my dorm while watching TV. "Stay close to me. That's the only way you are protected from Satan."

I cannot count the number of times I have fallen short of God's grace. "For all have sinned and fall short of the glory of God" (Rom. 3:23). "But God demonstrates His own love toward us, in that while we were still sinners, Christ died for us (Rom. 5:8). Most of the times that I messed up, I did not feel like repenting because something told me, "You are nothing, God will never forgive you or use someone like you. Do what everyone else is doing. Give up." That something was Satan.

Whenever Satan sees that you have a calling in your life, he uses every tactic he can to get you off track. Remember that he is the father of lies. Unfortunately for him, "Greater is He [Jesus] that is in you than he that's in the world [Satan] (1 John 4:4).

Holiness Still

The only way to be a vessel for God is to crucify your flesh daily. "If anyone desires to come after Me, let him deny himself, and take up his cross daily, and follow Me (Luke 9:23). In order for us to be more like Jesus, "He must increase, but I must decrease" (John 3:30).

When you surrender to God, in essence you are saying, "Lord, I want you to be in control of my life" letting God know that you are serious about your relationship with Him. Do not fight your own battles. What do I mean by fighting you own battles? For example, drug addicts who go to church regularly but are still grappling with drugs need God's help. However, if they do not pray and ask God for help but try to do it alone, they are fighting their own battles.

Surrendering to God is saying, "Lord, I need you to help me get rid of lying, cursing, and low-self esteem." Living holy is not easy. It can be challenging at times. Holiness is a commandment, not an option. The word of God tells us to, "Be **holy** because I, the LORD your God, am **holy** (Lev. 19:2, emphasis added).

I made a mistake

Making mistakes is something we all do on a regular basis. However, most people take two approaches. You have those who learn from their mistakes and those who criticize and discourage themselves after making a mistake.

In life, everyone is going to make mistakes. God understands that. Making a mistake lets you know what your strengths and weaknesses are. It lets you know the areas in your life that you need to work on. You will never know if there is a problem until you make a mistake.

You become wiser only if you learn from your mistake. Take that opportunity to work on it so that next time, you do not do the same thing over. I have heard people sometimes say, "I made the same mistake twice." That happens because they did not take their time to correct the first mistake. Let me exemplify what I mean.

For example, your math teacher gives you an equation to solve. She looks at it and said you did everything right except on the last step, you put x=two instead of x=five.

Two weeks later while taking the final, you see the same problem. This point is crucial because if you did not correct that mistake, you probably will put the same wrong answer as you did before. However, if you corrected it, you would not have any concerns.

Over the years, I have learned to be the first group. I used to be critical of myself whenever I made a mistake or did something wrong. I felt as if every time I tried to do something, I was going to mess up. I became afraid of messing up.

In order for God to get me to a place where I realized its okay to make mistake, He first had to make me realize that I am not perfect. Only He is.

As we go along our walk with God, there will be times when it seems as if everything we do or try to do is wrong. That lets you know that our imperfection is His Perfection. His strength perfects our weakness. Whenever you feel weary, ask God to strengthen you. He will.

The people that have a difficult time dealing with challenges in life are the second group. Those people beat themselves on the head after messing up; they feel ashamed. If you feel ashamed after doing something wrong, it is not of God. God puts guilt on us when we mess up and not shame because shame says, "I am something wrong" while guilt says, "I did something wrong." Do not beat yourself over the head every time you make a mistake.

Satan's goal is to get you discouraged so that you cannot destroy his kingdom. Life is too short and precious to beat yourself over the head every time you make a mistake. The devil will always bring your past to discourage you. Do not let that stop you from seeking God. Whenever Satan reminds you of your past, remind him of his Future— spending **eternity** in hell.

Chapter 8

Breaking it down

Being a Christian does not mean that you are always going to church. Unfortunately, many people have the misconception that Christians live boring lives. As Christians, we too can have fun. However, there are certain lines that the world crosses but we cannot cross. Where do we draw the line? How far is too far? Is it a sin to listen to secular music? These are some of the questions that I will touch on in this chapter. So keep reading.

A Word of Hope and Encouragement

Remember now your Creator in the days of your youth, before the difficult days come, and the years draw near when you say, I have no pleasure in them. (Eccl. 12:1).

Party Time

I am not a party pooper. Several people have asked me, "Is it wrong to go to a party or a club?" Before answering the question, I usually ask them what their motives are for going. Some say they just want to have fun, while others say they go just to hang out.

Having a Good Time

Life is not supposed to be boring as Christians. Some people think all we do is have Bible studies and pray in tongues all day. Christians like to have fun too, whether it consists of going out with friends or relaxing at home with family.

Is it wrong to party? Does the Bible say anything about partying or clubbing?

The Bible does not address this topic directly. However, it does give us adequate information on how to conduct ourselves. First, let us look at some scriptures.

I Corinthians 6:19-20 says, "Do you not know that your body is a **temple of the Holy Spirit**, who is in you, whom you have received from God? You are not your own; **you were bought at a price**. Therefore **honor** God with your body."(Emphasis added). Our body is a temple of the Holy Spirit. What exactly does that mean? Well let us define the word "temple."

A temple is something regarded as having within it a divine presence. In the Old Testament, before the priest could come into the presence of God (the Holy of Holies) he had to be pure and holy or else he died.

Jesus went into a temple in Jerusalem and was not pleased with what He saw.

"So they came to Jerusalem. Then Jesus went into the temple and began to drive out those who bought and sold in the temple, and overturned the tables of the money changers and the seats of those who sold doves. And He would not allow anyone to carry wares through the temple. Then He taught, saying to them, is it not written, My house shall be called a house of prayer for all nations? But you have made it a den of thieves" (Mark 11:15-17).

Whatever we do with our bodies, it must be pleasing unto the Lord. When you go to parties or clubs and start dancing, if Jesus were to walk into your temple, would He be pleased with it? When people go to parties or clubs and start dancing, they usually get close physically which causes certain physical sensations to be aroused. Because of that sensation, some people become sexually intimate.

We are to honor God with our bodies. God should always be pleased with what you do with and to your body. If you are dancing sexually with anyone, you allow Satan to come in your mind with sexual thoughts and feelings.

When Christ died on the cross for our sins, we were "bought at a price." In other words, your body is not your own anymore. He paid for it with His life.

One of the biggest mistakes most Christians make is that we think in order to have fun we have to sell ourselves or lower our standards. You can be a Christian and have fun without compromising your standards. God is calling every Christian to live Holy and pure. "Be **holy**, because I am **holy**" (Lev. 11:45, emphasis added).

Just hanging out

Some people like to hang out and meet people at parties. I myself like going to meet new people and make friends. However, there are several ways you can meet new people and make friends—school, church, and bus stops, just to name a few. Others like to go to parties just to "chill out," which is fine depending on who you are. Some people can be in certain environments and not be influenced while others cannot.

If you are a person who gets loose easily in this type of environment, then I would not advise putting yourself in such a compromising situation. It is not advisable for people to go to parties or clubs because the enemy knows how to get us when we think we have everything under control.

It is important to have a personal relationship with the Holy Spirit because He will guide you and lets you know what is good and not good for you. The next time plan on going to a party to chill or just to have "fun," ask yourself this question, "Am I going to honor God with my body?"

Listening to Secular Music

Is it okay to listen to secular music as Christians? Before answering that question, let us look at the origin of music.

There is no human activity more intriguing to angels than our making of music. The scripture gives enough information to understand how this all came about. Angels inhabit the Kingdom of Heaven and are counted among the heavenly host. They glorify His name with celestial singing that surpasses anything we have ever heard or will hear on earth. Can you imagine all the angels in heaven glorifying and giving praise to He who, "Made the earth, whose hands stretched out the heavens, and all their host has He commanded" (See Is. 45:12).

I wish I could see what the prophet Isaiah saw, "I saw the Lord seated on a throne, high and *exalted*" (Is. 6:1, emphasis added). Can you imagine the King of Kings and Lord of Lords worshiped forever? That gets me very excited. I cannot wait for that glorious day when we all get together, what a day of rejoicing that will be.

The Origin of Music

Lucifer (now known as Satan or the Devil) was one of three archangels (Michael and Gabriel being the other two), and no cherub or seraph was allowed closer proximity to the throne of God than these. As Heaven's choir director, it was Lucifer's responsibility to lead the angelic host in worship. Created with instruments of music fashioned into his being—"The workmanship of thy tabrets and of thy pipes was prepared in thee in the day that thou was created" (Ezek. 28:13). He not only conducted the orchestra, he *was* the orchestra. He had different sounds emanating from his body.

Not only was he the orchestra, he was very wise and extremely beautiful: "Every precious stone was thy covering, the Sardis, topaz, and the diamond, the beryl, the onyx, and the jasper, the sapphire, the emerald, and the carbuncle, and gold." Then in the midst of Heaven's order and harmony, "When the morning stars [angels] sang together, and all the sons of God shouted for joy" (Job 38:7), Lucifer saw his own beauty and brilliance and declared, "I will ascend into Heaven, I will exalt my throne above the stars [angels] of God; ... I will be like the most High." (Is. 14:13-14).

After a while, he became big headed. He fell in love with himself. He spent endless hours in gazing at the reflection of his awesome beauty. He endeared his beauty to himself in shaking each feather and watching it send bolts of lightening over the heads of the angels. He loved to impress them with his power and beauty. He fluttered his huge six wings in dancing, up and down; back and forth with each feather glowing like jewels and thundering like waterfalls. He loved the glitter of floor length hair that shone like lightning and He worshipped his broad chest and huge powerful body.

Lucifer loved his most beautiful face among all the angels, bold eyes, perfect lips, ears, gigantic six wings, his huge broad powerful chest, huge neck, broad shoulders and powerful legs and arms. He loved the respect of angels. He loved his voice and wanted it to be used not in singing and worshipping his Maker but in ordering God and the angels to obey him. In his pride and love for himself, he forgot completely that he is only a breath of God and not the Maker of angels, people, stars, and everything.

When Lucifer was cast to the earth "As lightning falls from heaven" with a third of the heavenly host (who by their free will chose to worship him as a god), he brought his talent for music with him. It follows that a contamination has infected the music on earth, for we have songs that glorify Satanic deception, rebellion, and the occult, driven into the mind and soul of the youth by instruments and amplifiers pushed to torturous sound levels; and thousands have given themselves in worship to "the god of this age."

Now that you have an idea where music originated, I will address the question I posed earlier, "Is it okay to listen to secular music as Christians?

In order to answer this question, I break secular music in these categories:

First category: There are secular songs without derogatory innuendo. That is, certain secular songs do not bring any negative thoughts, feelings, or emotions because of listening to them. These songs inspire and encourage you even though they are not talking about Jesus. Songs like this include, "I believe I can fly", "We are the World," and many others.

"I believe I can fly" encourages you to go after your dreams. "We are the world" talks about helping orphans and kids with AIDS in Africa. We can all agree that those are not only good things to do, but Christ would want us to do them as well.

Second Category: These secular songs cause Jesus to be the last person on your mind. You avoid listening to these songs or singing the lyrics with your youth pastor or parents around because you will get in trouble. For example, you cannot Listen to "Hot in here" by Nelly and think about the awesomeness of God's creation. "Shake it fast," "Thong song," "Back that thing up," are not songs to listen to because the lyrics have negative connotations. You do not have to shake anything for Jesus. Come as you are and He will receive you.

Songs like these do not feed your spirit but your flesh. It is important to remember what the scripture says, "Do not be deceived, God is not mocked; for whatever a man sows, that he will also reap. For he who sows to his flesh will of the flesh reap corruption, but he who sows to the Spirit will of the Spirit reap everlasting life (Gal. 6:7-8). Songs like these are not healthy for your spiritual growth. You cannot grow spiritually by infiltrating your mind with lyrics that have a derogatory connotation.

Third Category: There is controversy in the Christian community about love songs. Some Christians say that you should not listen to them while others say it is okay to listen to them. The Bible does not answer this question directly. However, 1 Corinthians 13, teaches us that God is love, suggesting that God is not against songs that simply talk about loving each other.

On the contrary, He is not so pleased about the way we misuse and abuse them. People always find a way to use what was meant to help us and turn it into something hurtful and meaningless.

When two people become one in holy matrimony, love songs have more meaning then only because when you are single you might hear a song that you like and call it "your song" and dedicate it to your significant other at the time. However, when you break up with that person, the last song you want to hear is what used to be "your song."

"I just listen to the beat!"

"I just listen to the beat" is the excuse many people use for listening to certain secular songs. Sadly, this it is one of the primary deceits the enemy uses to discombobulate people. It is amazing how people are able to memorize a rap album in the first week of its release but cannot quote a single Bible verse even if their life depended on it.

If we were to memorize Bible verses as much as we memorize these songs, we would have thousands of scriptures ready to combat the enemy's attack. I encourage you to make memorizing scriptures a habit.

Chapter 9

The Grace of God

Life can be full of surprises. Sometimes things happen to us that leave us speechless. Because of that, we get angry with God. Regardless of what happens to us as believers, God will never put more on us that we can handle. When your life is in His hands, you feel at ease.

A word of Hope and Encouragement

He who dwells in the secret place of the Most High shall abide under the shadow of the almighty. I will say of the Lord, "He is my refuge and my fortress; My God, in Him I will trust." Surely, He shall deliver you from the snare of the fowler and from the perilous pestilence. He shall cover you with His feathers, and under His wings, you shall take refuge; his truth shall be your shield and buckler. You shall not be afraid of the terror by night, nor of the arrow that flies by day, nor of the pestilence that walks in darkness, nor of the destruction that lays waste at noonday. (Ps. 91:1-6)

Friendships

Growing up, I did not have many friends. I had people I associated with but I did not call them friends. After seeing what they did, it discouraged me from pursuing a friendship with them. My parents taught me that, "Evil company corrupts good habits."

Throughout my childhood, I was always by myself. It seemed like whenever I tried to "get down" with the crowd, I felt out of place. Being a loner is not for everybody because some people like to be doing something every minute. It drives them crazy to be by themselves. However, for me, that was to my advantage because that is how I learned the importance of spending time with God.

I remember praying for God to send me friends, people that I could trust. One of the kids who grew up on my block—Steven Reeves—became my good friend. I thank God for putting him on my path. We encouraged each other in the Lord. Today, he is one of the few people I call a friend.

Stanley and I used to play basketball in the park when we were kids. I never talked to him because He was one of those kids your parents told you not to hang around.

One day while in English class, we were asked to work with a partner on an assignment. Stanley and I ended up working together. As we worked on the paper, we started talking about God. I was surprise to hear him talking about God because I did not know that he was also a Christian.

He and I have a special friendship. I knew him when he was the old Stanley, and he knew me when I was the shy and quiet boy. He is like a brother to me. He has my back and I have his.

Friendship is something that everyone needs. The relationship I have with Stanley and Steve as well as other people is important to me. I would not trade our friendship for any amount of money in the world.

If you want God to send you friends, pray for them as well as show yourself friendly. Pray for friends that will always be by your side. This kind of friendship is important because you have someone as your accountability partner. It is difficult to be going through something and not have anyone to help you get through it.

He is always there for you

Whenever I hear a story that inspires me or motivates me, I love to share it with people hoping it will do the same for them. The story I am going to share with you encouraged me and hopefully it will do the same for you.

There was a pastor in a small town who received a call from one of his church members late at night. One of his member's houses was robbed. In a hurry, the pastor took his jacket and rushed to go see if everything was all right.

On his way there, he came across a man standing in an alley. The man asked him if he had a match with him, the pastor happened to have some with him. He gave it to the man and walked away.

The following morning, while watching the news, the pastor saw the man on the police custody. He wondered why. To his surprise, the man had killed two people that night he met the pastor and he was looking for his third victim. He was a serial killer on the loose.

This bothered the pastor because the man did not kill or try to hurt him. Therefore, he decided to go to the police station where the man was to talk to him.

When he arrived, he told the police about his encounter he had with the man. The warned him not to go near the man because he was a serial killer. However, the pastor insisted on briefly speaking with the man.

The pastor asks the man, "Why didn't you kill me or hurt me?" The man looked at the preacher and said, "When you gave me the match, after lighting it, I saw two angels standing next to you and I couldn't do anything." The man of God was speechless. "The angel of the LORD **encamps** around those who fear him, and he delivers them" (Ps. 34:7, emphasis added).

It is awesome to know that as believers, we have the angels of the Lord on our side. The God we serve is always there to protect us from the evil one. God protects us from many things without us being aware of it. Look at the preacher for example; he had no idea that the man saw angels besides him.

When Satan looks at a child of God, he does not see us. He sees instead the, "Lamb of God, who takes away the sin of the world" (John 1:29). Can you imagine what would have happened to that man of God? He probably would have been dead also.

However, the "Lamb of God" sent His angels to encamp around his servant. To God be all the Glory and Honor!

Run for your life

One day I went to hang out with Stanley at another friend's house. We ate, talked, and played Madden—the video game (for the record, I won every game).

It was getting late and almost time to go home. We talked about our favorite subjects other than God—girls. As we sat in his car conversing, a black Dodge Intrepid passed by. We did not think anything of it.

A few minutes later, we saw a police car driving towards us. The officer parked on the side, walked out of his car, and came to our car. He pointed his flashlights at us and told us to get out of the car. We were surprised because we did not know what was going on. He took both our licenses and ran them. After checking them, he told us everything was okay and to be careful.

The officer told us he did that because one of the neighbors had called the police and said that someone was about to rob his house. Therefore, he thought that might have been us.

The black car that had passed by us the first time came back. This time, it stopped beside out car. There were two men in the car. We both knew something was about to happen. If you grew up in the 'hood' and a car pulled by you with tinted windows late at night, you knew that was your cue to run for your life and ask questions later.

A man walked out of the car and reached on his side to pull a gun. Our hearts dropped as we saw our lives flashed before our eyes. Stanley put the car in reverse and drove backwards without looking behind. The man chased us as we drove. Suddenly, he stopped and ran back to his car to follow us.

Stanley crashed the car into a big tree because of nervousness. The impact damaged the rear of the car, breaking the window. We both jumped out the car and ran behind bushes.

We called 911. "Send the police, someone is trying to kill us," we told the operator. We ran behind people's yards and bushes.

I had never been that terrified in my life. I saw my whole life flashing before my eyes. In the middle of this, I said, "Lord I can't die now without getting married, please don't let me die". I did not care about anything else but getting married. I thought about all the things I wanted to do that I have not had the opportunity to do.

Somehow, Stanley and I separated. I went behind someone's house and hid myself in the bushes. I took my white shirt and sneakers off because of the visibility. I did not know where Stanley was. I did not want to call him because they would have heard my voice. Therefore, I sat there quiet and prayed. I prayed for God to send the police and to keep Stanley safe as well.

After about twenty minutes, (it felt like hours), I saw the police lights flashing. I immediately jumped out the bushes and ran towards the police car without my shirt and holding my sneakers.

The officers told me to stop running, sit down, and relax. I was breathing intensely. I was glad to see that Stanley was okay.

One of the officers asked me if I wanted him to call the ambulance. I said no because I was not sure if I had insurance.

At the time of the incident, I felt the impact but I did not feel the pain. The following morning, I could barely move my neck around.

If it were not for God's protection, I probably would have been in the hospital or dead. However, because of Him, I was saved. Never in a million years would I have thought something like that was going to happen to me, but it did. I was not afraid of dying and going to hell. I was more afraid of dying and not getting married. I knew that if I died, I would be in heaven with my Lord because to be absent from the body is to present with the Lord. I did not want my life to end that way. In addition, I was also hungry and did not want to die and go to heaven hungry. I would have been one angry and hungry black man in heaven. I think God would have understood.

Just call on Jesus

There is something powerful about that name—Jesus. Whenever you are going through a difficult time, call on Jesus. In the midst of your storm, when the red sea is in front of you and pharaoh's army is behind you, call on Jesus. If you do not feel well in your body and need a miracle, cry out Jesus. When you are going through challenges and you do not feel like praying, call on Jesus.

When you call on Jesus, your circumstance changes, when you cry out Jesus, demons tremble. When you cry out Jesus, the pain in your body goes away. When you cry out Jesus, you get delivered and set free from infirmities and deformities. If you can have only one word in your vocabulary, that word should be Jesus.

"At the name of Jesus **every knee** should bow, in heaven and on earth and under the earth, and **every tongue** should confess that Jesus Christ is Lord, to the glory of God the Father" (Phil. 2:10-11, emphasis added).

Do you need a miracle? Are you going through something and need extra help from God? Do you feel lost, confused, and depressed? I challenge you to call on Jesus. When you call on Jesus, your situation and circumstance will change.

Satan hates it when you call on the name of Jesus. When you say Jesus, you are saying, "**Greater is He** [Jesus] that's in me than he that's in the world" (1 John 4:4). When you say Jesus you saying, "**I can do all things** through Christ who strengthens me" (Philippians 4:13, emphasis added). When you say Jesus you are saying, "N**o weapon** formed against you shall prosper" (Is. 54:17, emphasis added). When you say Jesus, you are saying that you might be "hard pressed on every side, but not crushed; perplexed, but not in despair; persecuted, but not abandoned; struck down, but not destroyed" (2 Cor. 4:8,9). When you know the God that you serve, you have no reason to be afraid of anything or anyone.

He is the First and Last, the Beginning and the End. He always was, He always is, and He always will be unmoved, unchanged, undefeated, and never undone.

In fact, He is so great that the world cannot understand him, the armies cannot defeat Him, the schools cannot explain Him, Herod could not kill Him, the leaders cannot ignore Him, and Donahue cannot explain Him.

When you fall, He lifts you up! When you fail, He forgives; when you are weak, He is strong. His strength perfects our weakness. When you are afraid, He is your encourager. When you are confused, He counsels you. When you stumble and fall (we fall down but we get up), He keeps you steady. When you are heartbroken, he mends your broken heart. When you are hurt, He is your healer. When you did not have anything to eat, He fed you. When your world was crashing down on you, He was besides you. When you faced problems and went through pain, He comforted you. Moreover, when you face death, He is going to carry you Home where you will not have to worry about pain or sickness. All you have to do is enjoy.

Jesus Christ has been given all authority in heaven and on earth. The next time you are in trouble and need extra help, just call on Jesus and He will set you free. Thank God for Jesus!

Chapter 10

It SHALL come to pass

One the hardest thing to do as a believer is to wait on the Lord. Sometimes, God delays our blessings in order to teach us about the importance of waiting on Him. If you are grappling in this area, pray and ask God to help you. If God has promised you something but the waiting period seems too long, do not give up. God's delays are not denials.

A word of Hope and Encouragement

So shall My word that goes forth from My mouth; it shall not return to Me void, but it shall accomplish what I please, and it shall prosper in the thing for which I sent it. (Is. 55:11)

Patience

Have you ever waited for weeks, months, or even years to get something you desired? After waiting for a while, you get mad, frustrated, and aggravated because time seems to be going by slowly. Sometimes it seems like it is too long and you tell God that you do not even want it anymore. Does that sound familiar?

No one likes to wait for anything. I hated having to wait for something I wanted. If I wanted something, I wanted it then or never. I remember asking my dad, "Can I borrow your camera to take pictures with my friends at school?"

"No!"

"Why not?" I asked him.

"You'll mess it up," he replied.

I was furious. I grumbled and grumbled, but that did not make any difference. That year while opening my Christmas gifts, to my surprise, he bought me a camera. I was happier I received it for Christmas than before. That is how it is with God.

Sometimes when we ask God for things, He will either give it to us, or make us wait. Even though His word encourages us to "ask and ye shall be given," that does not mean that you will get it automatically.

Unfortunately, too many people give up on their blessings before they receive them. Patience works for our own good.

"And we know that all things work together for the good to those who love God, to those who are called according to His purpose" (Rom. 8:28). Patience produces several fruits. Perseverance and maturity are just a couple.

Perseverance

Patience can be defined as steadiness, endurance, or perseverance in performing tasks. It took me quite a while to comprehend this. I had to learn that if I wanted to be an effective Christian, I could not do so without having patience. When you are patient, it shows God that you are maturing. Moreover, regardless of what comes your way, you are not going to waiver, but stand strong.

Jeremiah 29:11 says, "For I know the thoughts I think towards you, says the Lord, thoughts of peace and not of evil, to give you a future and a hope." Though I could not see the promises of God manifesting in my life at times because of my surroundings, I had to be patient and let God work things out on His timetable, not mine. Satan does not like people who are patient. He knows that if you wait on God and not give up, God will answer our prayers. "**Wait on the Lord**; be of good courage, And He shall strengthen your heart; Wait, I say, on the Lord" (Ps. 27:14, emphasis added).

You cannot resist the enemy if you are not patient. Patience tells Satan that in spite of your situation you will wait on the Lord. "He gives power to the weak, and to those who have no might He increases strength. Even the youth shall faint and be weary, and the young men shall utterly fall. **But** those who wait on the Lord shall renew their strength; they shall mount up with wings like eagles, they shall run and not be wary, they shall walk and not faint (Is. 40:29-31, emphasis added).

As I briefly mentioned earlier, patience also shows maturity. Mature believers understand the important of waiting on the Lord. They have seen how God rewards them for their patience. It takes a time get to that point, but once you get there, it a blessing. In addition, you will be able to help others as well.

As I matured in my walk with God (and I am still maturing), I learned to, "**Wait on the Lord**, be of good courage and He shall strengthen your heart; Wait, I say, on the Lord" (Ps. 27:14, emphasis added).

After seeing the results of being patient, I stopped rushing God. There were times I saved myself the drama by waiting on God. On the other hand, there were also times I did not save myself the drama by not waiting on God.

Are you struggling with waiting on the Lord? Do God's promises seem to be taking forever? Remember that whenever God promises something, it shall come to pass. Nothing and no one can stop it.

"For My thoughts are not your thoughts, nor are your ways my ways, says the LORD. For as the heavens are higher than the earth, so are my ways higher than your ways, and my thoughts than your thoughts. For as the rain comes down, and the snow from heaven, and do not return there, but water the earth, and make it bring forth and bud, that it may give seed to the sower and bread to the eater, so shall My word be that goes forth from My mouth; it shall not return to Me void, but it shall accomplish what I please, and it shall prosper in the things for which I sent it" (Is. 55:10-11).

If you struggle in this area, ask God to help you. You can pray, "Dear Heavenly father, I have a problem waiting on you. I do not know how to wait on you according to your word. Give me patience and teach me how to be of good courage while I wait on your promises for my life, in the name of Jesus. Amen."

Chapter 11

He met me

When you are hungry for the presence of God, it shows God that you are serious about Him. Many of us are used to always asking God for something. When you start asking God for His presence and not just His blessings, your life will never be the same.

A word of Hope and Encouragement

If anyone desires to come after Me, let him deny himself, and take up his cross daily, and follow Me. (Luke 9:23)

Friday night service

One Friday night, I went to an evening prayer service at my church. While I was praying, God started speaking to me. He said that there was a strong demonic presence in the building and the children of God were under attack.

As the prayer became intense, the Lord said His people had won the victory. I could feel the presence intensified as we prayed.

After service, I found out that there was a possessed woman in the service. However, as the prayer *intensified*, she left the service. That is when I understood what the Lord meant by "there is a strong demonic presence."

The presence of the Lord

I love spending time in the presence of the Lord because I experience His glory and power. One night, I felt the presence of God in a mighty way.

Before going to bed, I got on knees and started praying. Then the presence of God filled my room. As I prayed, I felt His powerful presence. I felt as if I was about to explode because of the power of the presence. A bright light filled my room. I seemed to have stepped into Heaven.

As I looked in the Spirit, I saw a bright light shining down on me. I felt as if my roof was lifted and the light was coming through. The more I prayed, the more the presence intensified. I felt like the Prophet Elijah when he was caught up in Glory. I do not know how long it lasted. I do know one thing; God met me that night in a glorious way. Oh! How wonderful it is to fellowship with the Living God. There is nothing like it!

Chapter 12

Calling my name

We are living in the end time. God is looking for people (especially young people) to use for His Glory. My prayer is that you will allow God to use you without asking for your permission. When you let Him use you, the sky is the limit. As you read this chapter, read it with an open heart and mind. Let the precious Holy Spirit minister to you.

A word of Hope and Encouragement

Let no one despise your youth, but be an example to the believers in word, in conduct, in love, in spirit, in faith, in purity. (1 Tim. 4:12)

Who is calling me?

One evening while praying, God said that He was going to reveal hell to me. I was afraid because I had just finished reading "A Divine Revelation of Hell" by Mary K. Baxter and it was intensely scary. After reading that book, I prayed with my lights one for one week.

The following day, while taking a nap, I heard a voice calling me, "Mathew." I quickly glanced outside the window but did not see anyone so I went back to sleep.

A few minutes later, I heard the same voice again calling, "Mathew." My heart was beating fast because I heard someone calling me but could not see whom it was or know exactly where it was coming from. Something like this had never happened to me before. I could tell the voice was not an ordinary voice. I felt peace when heard the voice.

After looking around and not seeing anyone, I went back to sleep again.

As I pursued the Lord, He revealed other things to me. He said, "All the things I am showing (and will continue to show you) you are to write it down and tell My people". That is exactly what I am doing, telling His people.

He spoke to me

The presence and the power of God fell mightily one specific Sunday morning in church. Everyone was weeping. As I stood there, God spoke to me. I did not know what to do because that was the first time He gave me a prophetic word to give in a public setting. I was nervous about how people would receive it. Would they think I was crazy? In addition, I was a new member at this church.

After battling with this for a few minutes, I decided to let it out regardless of what happened.

As I spoke, a couple of the brothers from the church came, held me, and took me in another room. I was angry and wondered why they did that. One of the brothers explained to me that the word (even though was from God) was harsh.

Every time I prophesied, I was told the words I gave were accurate but harsh. At the time, I could not understand why.

What they meant by harsh and forceful was that even though the prophetic words were accurate, I did not give the word in a receivable manner. God was working on my character (and He still is). It is difficult to be an ambassador for God without a godly character.

I hated that period of my life because it was difficult and painful. Everyone told me the same thing. I became frustrated at myself and with others.

In order to be a person of integrity, you need to let God complete the work He has started in you—a process many leaders do not complete. To my surprise, building a godly character was not something that came overnight.

I have seen several people with the talent, the potential, and the gifts. However, they were missing one important thing—a respectful character. People like this will never get anywhere in life because it is difficult for them to maintain healthy relationships.

On the contrary, there are those with outstanding character. Whenever you are around them, you feel encouraged, loved, and respected. God is looking for people with character to represent Him.

I heard Him

As I grew in my walk with God, He started speaking to me about things I needed to change in my life. One day after praying, something amazing happened. I had an open vision (my eyes were open but I could see things as if there where happening in front of me).

In the vision, I saw the Spirit of the Lord being poured out in a great measure to my generation. Then I heard the Spirit of the Lord saying, "Arise, for the Battle is on." I saw a large crowd of youth fighting a spiritual battle, thousands upon thousands. I also saw angels of the Lord working side by side with the youth to defeat Satan. Then I saw The Lord pouring out his strength to those who were getting weary. Isaiah 40:29-31 came to mind:

"He gives power to the weak, and to those who have no might He increases strength. Even the youths shall faint and be weary, and the young men shall utterly fall, **but those who wait** on the LORD shall renew their strength; they shall mount up with wings like eagles, they shall run and not be weary, they shall walk and not faint." (Emphasis added)

Here is the prophecy:

For the Spirit of the Lord has been poured out even more on the young people of this generation. In the seasons past, my young people have been despised, abused, and ignored. However, this is a new generation; a generation that I will work great signs and wonders through.

Church, do not despise your youth. The Lord your God is getting ready to do something great with them. Young people, this is the season, says the Lord, that you will find Me when you search for Me with all your heart.

In the seasons past, many of you have been asking, "Where are you, Lord?" The Lord your God is right here; I hide from you because you did not search for me with all your heart. Get ready, get ready, get ready, says the Lord of Hosts.

There is too much division among God's people. Can we all get along as children of God? God has given me such a burden to see the young people serving Him. The Lord spoke to me again and said:

"There is an even greater war for the young people of this generation. This is the time for the youth to get together. Do not say to your friend, because you are not part of my church I will not part with you. For this is the time, says the Lord, that I will bring together all my young people to get them ready for battle. You have to be ready to fight the enemy. Out of every corner of the earth, men of God are being raised. Young men that will lead my people to victory; men that will listen to my commands, men that will come out of their comfort zone and take a stand for Me.

For even right now, I am raising young women that will be the mothers of my house. Get ready young women, for the task I am about to give you. The Lord your God has raised you up for this reason—to shepherd the people of God.

I am raising young men that will go to the streets and preach my word. Do not worry about how the gospel will be preached on the streets, for the Lord your God has already made a way. The young people that I raised will be well equipped; they will not be defeated because the Lord your God has given them the victory. I will raise and send those people that others never thought could do it, those that have been broken hearted, and those that have been abused. I am not racist; I do not look at the color of your skin but at the openness of your heart. So open your heart to me, young people, and let Me use you. This is your season and your time, your season and your time says the Lord."

Those that have an ear to hear will hear what the Spirit is saying to the churches.

Chapter 13

While I was in the Spirit

It is only through the Spirit of the Living God that we can see the supernatural realm. I am amazed about the reality of the spirit realm. Many people do not take it seriously.

In this chapter, God revealed some things to me in the supernatural. I hope that after reading this chapter you will ask God to open your spiritual eyes so that you, too, can see in the Spirit.

A word of Hope and Encouragement

In the year that King Uzziah died, I saw the Lord sitting on a throne, high and lifted up, and the train of His robe filled the temple. Above it stood seraphim; each one had six wings: with two, he covered his face, with two, he covered his feet, and with two, he flew. And one cried to another and said: Holy, holy, holy is the Lord of hosts; the whole earth is full of His glory. (Is. 6:1-3)

The Revelations

I had a dream when I was in the fourth or fifth grade. This dream was not like any other dream I ever had.

In the dream, I was inside of a house. This house was not like any I had ever seen. The house had three sections. The first part had a long bleacher with people sitting on them. To my left, there was a window. Behind that window, I saw a creature that looked like a beast burning in a lake of intense fire. The creature was in excruciating agony. Even though I was standing by the window, I could not feel the heat but I could see the fire.

In front of me, there was an empty room. In that house, all the rooms were together. However, you could not go from one section of the room to another. There was a huge space, separating each room.

All of a sudden, I heard "Mathew." Someone called me from the empty room. Supernaturally, I disappeared and appeared to where I heard the voice. I looked but I could not see anyone. It felt as if I was in a forest and heard someone calling my name but I could not see who called me.

"You will help defeat the devil for Me and My son Jesus will help you." the voice said. When I turned, Jesus Christ was standing next to me. He looked at me and smiled. At that time, I was too young to understand what had just happened. This was the beginning of the revelations.

I wondered why He (Jesus) did not appear to me in His Glory. It was not until I became a teenager that I understood the revelation.

The Lord told me that the reason why I saw Him without his Glory was to let me know that He was one hundred percent human (and God). His birth, death, and resurrection are real.

I cannot believe that I had the opportunity to stand next to the King of Kings and Lord of Lords. I even touched Him. I touched the Master, the Great Healer that healed the sick and raised the dead. He was there with me. I saw the holes on His hands.

Seeking God

A few years went by before I had another dream similar to the one I just mentioned.

I was standing in a parking lot (I had no clue where I was), when a Man appeared to me. When I looked at Him, I shouted, "You are Jesus, the Man I saw in my dream when I was eight years old." I hugged Him because I was excited to see Him again. He looked at me but did not say anything. The look on His face said, "I know you did." I was excited and did not know what to do. Here I was again with the Prince of Peace, standing and talking to Him. I could not believe it.

When I first saw Him as a child, I knew of Him and not about Him. This time, I was older and had learned more about Him.

As I stood there with the Master, I asked Him as many questions as I could about my future. He simply looked at me and did not utter a word. Oh! How I wish you too could have an encounter with the Master!

After talking to Him for a while He said, "Touch my side, where I was pierced. Touch the holes in my hands where I was nailed." With tears in my eyes I said, "Lord, I can't do it; I don't want to do it." "Here, put your hands on my hands and on my side." With nervousness and weeping, I took my right hand and gently touch His side; the place where they pierced him was deep. The holes in his hands frightened me because of how large the holes were. All of a sudden, He disappeared. Then I remembered what the prophet Isaiah said this:

"Who has believed our report? And to whom has the arm of the Lord been revealed? For he shall grow up before Him as a tender plant, and as a root out of dry ground. He has no form or comeliness; and when we see Him, there is no beauty that we should desire Him. He is despised and rejected by men, a Man of sorrows and acquainted with grief. And we hid, as it were, our faces from Him; he was despised, and we did not esteem Him. Surely, He has borne our griefs and carried our sorrows; yet we esteemed Him stricken, smitten by God, and afflicted. **But He was wounded for our transgressions, He was bruised for our iniquities; The chastisement for our peace was upon Him, and by His stripes we are healed.** All we like sheep have gone astray; We have turned, every one, to his own way; and the Lord has laid on Him the iniquity of us all. He was oppressed and He was afflicted, yet He opened not His mouth; He was led as a lamb to the slaughter, and as a sheep before its shearers is silent, so He opened not His mouth. He was taken from prison and from judgment, and who will declare His generation? For he was cut off from the land of the living. For the transgressions of My people was stricken. And they made His grace with the wicked, But with the rich at His death because he had done no violence, nor was any deceit in His mouth. Yet it pleased the Lord to bruise him" (Is. 53:1-10, emphasis added).

The Face

A friend of mine once invited me to his youth group. Before going, I decided to take a nap. While taking a nap, I noticed something strange. As I turned on my bed, I saw a round face. It was as though a cloud had formed to make this face. The face was like that of a ghost. I though I was imaging things so I turned the opposite direction to make sure that it was not my imagination.

When I turned back to the side I originally saw the face, it was still there. This time, the face became fuller and more realistic. I could not believe it.

That night while praying, the Lord revealed to me that He was opening my spiritual eyes and showing me things in the Spirit I had never seen. I saw things in the spirit without being aware of it. The Spirit of God revealed Himself to me that afternoon.

Pray, and ask Him to do the same for you. Trust me, He will.

Why me Lord?

I did not understand why I was seeing revelation after revelation. During that season, I heard the audible voice of God the Father, saw God the Son, felt the presence of God the Holy Spirit like never before, had angelic visitations and had a revelation of hell. One day I asked the Lord why He was showing me all these revelations. What had I done to deserve such favor? He gave me part of the reason why.

I heard the Holy Spirit say, "When you seek me with all your heart, you will find me." God is now more than ever looking for individuals that will not stop seeking Him until they see His face. People are always seeking the hand of God and not his face.

Another reason is that He wanted me to tell the world that His Birth, Death, and Resurrection is real. "Tell my people that you saw Me. Tell them that my death and resurrection was real. I came to die for the lost, to give hope to those without hope."

Do you want to see the face of God? Do you need a revelation that only God can give you? All you have to do is seek Him with all your heart and you will find Him. "Then you will call upon Me and go and pray to Me, and I will listen to you. And you will seek Me and find Me, when you search for Me with all your heart" (Jer. 29:12-14).

The tunnel

After praying one night, I laid down to sleep. A few seconds later, my Spirit left my body. I found myself going down a tunnel. While going down the tunnel, it became brighter. I had no clue where I was or going or what was going on. I saw people as far ahead as I could see, thousands upon thousands of people.

Finally, when I enter what looked like the heart of tunnel, I saw disturbing images. The thousands of people I saw were bound with chains as the lake of fire burned them. From the expression on their faces, they seem to be in agony. It was sad and disturbing to me.

When I looked up, the top of the tunnel was open. Through that opening I saw a bright light shining into the tunnel. Somehow, I was elevated to the top of the tunnel to see where the light was coming from. The light was as bright as the sun. I could tell from the distance that the light was coming from a farther distance. That is when I realized that the tunnel was bright because of the light.

Suddenly, I found myself back down on the heart of the tunnel. I was surprised about what happened. How was I elevated to the top of the tunnel and brought back down? There was a big gap separating the bottom from the top. I saw people stepping on top of each other struggling to get to the light. Unfortunately, they could not because it was too late. It was not a beautiful picture.

The horror, agony, and suffering brought tears to my eyes. Some of those people had the opportunity to accept Jesus Christ as their lord and savior but they refused. The sad part about it is that they could not get out of hell regardless of how hard they tried. Satan and his "boys" did not allow them.

When I turned, I saw a huge black beast in front of me. The evil creature must have been twelve to fifteen feet tall. I have never seen anyone or anything as tall and ugly like that in my life. It fit the description of the beast talked about throughout the book of Revelation. All of a sudden, I was back in my room. It happened fast.

I will go

That night, for hours I cried to the Lord and said, "God wherever you send me to preach the Gospel I will go. I don't want another soul to go to hell." I felt his love even for those that rejected Him, those who were given the opportunity to receive salvation but turned it down. Please, do not let that be you. If you feel a tug in your heart, do not fight it. This could be your last chance. Tomorrow is not promised to anyone. Do not worry; you will be given an opportunity to accept Christ as your Lord and savior. Keep reading.

Establishing God's kingdom

A few months after seeing that vision, I had another dream. During the time of this dream, I was on a 40 days fast, seeking the face of God. I was desperate and hungry for a touch from God.

While taking a nap one afternoon, I found myself in a place covered with clouds. It was bright and empty. Then I heard a voice saying, "You shall establish my Kingdom." The voice was thunderous. I looked but I could not see anyone. I said, "What do you mean, Lord?" "You shall be My people and I will be your God." I was uncertain about what He meant. "What do you mean, Lord?" I asked again. "To have Me come and live in you."

That is when I woke up. Even after waking up, I still felt His presence. My eardrums vibrated as if someone had rung a loud bell next to them. My body vibrated for hours.

The Lord told me to share this with His people to let them know that He is real, and He still speaks to people.

Many people believe that God only spoke to those in the Bible. He did; but He did not stop there. He speaks to anyone willing to listen. Are you listening?

Chapter 14

Anointing fall on me

When Jesus ascended to Heaven, He sent us the precious Holy Spirit to be our counselor, comforter, and to guide us in all truths. Having an encounter with the precious Holy Spirit will change your life.

One summer during my junior year in high school, I had an encounter with the precious Holy Spirit that changed my life forever. I hope that you will let Him do the same for you.

A word of Hope and Encouragement

And it shall come to pass afterward that I will pour out My Spirit on all flesh; your sons and your daughters shall prophesy, your old men shall dream dreams, your young men shall see visions. And also on My menservants and on My maidservants I will pout out My Spirit in those days. And I will show wonders in the heavens and in the earth: Blood and fire and pillars of smoke. (Joel 2:28-30)

Camp Winburn

The day I received the baptism of the Holy Spirit, my life changed. That year, I heard about a camp in Maryland that was sponsored by my church (at that time). I thought it was a good idea to go and check it out. I called my pastor's wife (Sis Glynis) and told her that I wanted to go.

The follow morning she took me to the train station, bought my ticket, put me on the train, and contacted the camp director to come and pick me up from the train station. I was excited to go because I wanted to meet new people and make new friends.

When I arrived at the train station, the camp director took me to the campground. When we arrived at the campground, I felt lonely because I was the only kid from New Jersey and did not know anyone besides the camp director. However, after the first night, I made some friends.

The second night of camp, the speaker asked all those that want to be filled with the Holy Spirit to come to the altar so that she could pray for them. I was sitting in the back with a hot girl I met. I felt a nudge in my heart to go to the altar. I hesitated because I did not want to fall on the ground like everyone else and have that girl thinking I was crazy. A few minutes later, I felt an even stronger push.

Finally, I decided to go and stand in line to be prayed for. The song sang was, "Anointing fall on me." The speaker asked people to sing into the microphone, and as they started singing, she gently laid hands on them and the power of God knocked them to the ground.

As I stood in line, I prayed, "Lord I want to be filled with your Holy Spirit, Holy Spirit fill me up." When it was my turn to get on the microphone, I was somewhat hesitant about singing. I walk to the microphone and attempted to sing. The moment I said, "Anointing fall on me," the power of God fell on me and knocked me on the ground. I was vibrating all over the place. My arms, head, and legs were all over the place. After about forty-five minutes, my counselor had to walk me to my cabin.

The following morning, I was in pain. My head, arms, and legs were all in pain. Despite the pain, I would not trade that experience for anything else in the world. In fact, if I could do it all over again, I would.

The difficulties

I thought that everything was going to be a piece of cake after I was filled with the Holy Spirit. However, when I went home, I realized that things were much harder than I had anticipated.

What I did not know is that after you are filled with the Holy Spirit, you are put in the front line of God's army, and those are the ones the enemy goes after first. Even though I was filled with the Holy Spirit, I was not living a Spirit-filled life. I started watching things I was not supposed to watch and listened to songs that did not glorify God. I struggled with the things teenagers struggle with—lust, masturbation, pornography, etc. I was amazed that these issues became more eminent after I was baptized in the Spirit.

Being filled with the Holy Spirit does not make Satan afraid of you. Instead, you are the one he wants to get his hands on. I was not familiar with these scriptures:

In Ephesians 6:10-13, Paul said, "Finally, my brethren, be strong in the Lord and in the power of His might. Put on the whole armor of God, that you may be able to stand against the wiles of the devil. For we do not wrestle against flesh and blood, but against principalities, against powers, against the rulers of the darkness of this age, against spiritual hosts of wickedness in the heavenly places. Therefore, take up the whole armor of God, that you may be able to withstand in the evil day, and having done all, to stand." Philippians 4:13 "I can do all things through Christ who strengthens me." 1 John 4:4."Greater is He that's in me than He that's in the World." I was not taught how to use scriptures against the enemy.

New place

A few months after I had that encounter with the Holy Spirit, my family moved to another church. We loved our new church and decided to become members.

This church had more opportunity to grow in your faith. They had a teaching class called the school of the Holy Spirit. I was encouraged by my youth leader to take the class.

When the school of the Holy Spirit started, I went to their first meeting being skeptical of what to expect. The pastor in charge talked about the person of the Holy Spirit as well as His importance in our lives as believers. This was new and exciting to me. I knew very little about the Holy Spirit other than He was part of the Trinity.

After teaching, he asked everyone to stand and welcome the presence of the Lord. We all stood up and started praying. As I prayed, I felt the power of God on me strongly. I started jumping, shouting, and screaming violently. Another pastor and a deacon came over and held me. The pastor in charge came over and started praying. I remember him saying, "Be free in the name of Jesus, devil I command you to come out of him in the name of Jesus." The more he said that the more I vibrated and jumped. Then he said, "Be still in Jesus' name". As soon he said that, I was calm. I was scared because everything was new to me.

After calming down, I was taken into one of offices to be prayed for by another pastor and a deacon.

The Holy Spirit touched me that evening. When I went home, I got down on my knees and started praying. A few minutes later, my mom walked in my room and started prophesying, telling me that I need to get right with God. At that time, I was going through so much. I needed deliverance.

The Lord said to me through her, "You have the desire to serve me but your heart is not clean." After she prayed for me, I was delivered.

The following day, I felt refreshed and energetic. It was not until after my deliverance that I understood what the pastor meant by, "Be free in Jesus' name." You cannot serve God with an unclean heart.

Two weeks after I was delivered, I went back to the school of the Holy Spirit not being sure of what to expect this time. The topic for this class was how to know the Holy Spirit intimately.

After the class, I went home and started praying, telling the Lord that I wanted to get to know Him more intimately. The power of God fell on me and I started prophesying, something I had never done before. I had no clue what was going on. God was speaking through me. This was strange to me. I doubted if it was my voice or the voice of God. As soon as that thought came to mind, the Lord spoke and said, "Yes it is me, your God. You asked for me, now worship me," I kept on praying. As I prayed, the presence intensified. I felt released and burden free.

During this time, I could not wait to go home and pray after school. I rushed home from school just to pray. My relationship with God improved immensely. I felt much closer to God than before.

Chapter 15

The Spirit of the Living God

As believers, we need to understand the importance of the Holy Spirit in our lives. We need to understand that He is a person, not an "it," or a "thing." When I understood the revelation about the Holy Spirit being a person, my spiritual walk changed for the better. My prayer is that after reading this chapter, you too will be able to understand the precious Holy Spirit better. The precious Holy Spirit is also God.

A word of Hope and Encouragement

But the Helper, the Holy Spirit, whom the Father will send in My name, He will teach you all things, and bring to your remembrance all things that I said to you. (John 14:26)

He touched me

All my life I heard about Benny Hinn and how God uses him mightily. People said signs and wonders followed his ministry.

One day while watching TBN, I saw his crusade on TV. At the end of his show, he announced that he was going to be coming to Continental Airline Arena in New Jersey. I was excited because I had been hearing about this awesome man of God and I wanted to experience what I saw on TV and heard people talked about.

When we arrived, the choir was rehearsing praise and worship songs. My excitement grew. Besides looking forward to the power of God, I wanted to see him in person. The arena was filled with people from diverse backgrounds.

After praise and worship ended, many people that were healed from sicknesses and diseases were brought on stage to testify. I saw wheelchairs being brought up to the stage. Immediately, I said, "God that is how I want your presence to be evident in my ministry."

Benny Hinn later came out and started teaching about the Holy Spirit. As he spoke about the Holy Spirit, I felt His Presence the more.

When I looked at my family and crowd, everyone was worshipping God. I started weeping. I wept for two reasons: First, I told the Lord that I wanted to affect my generation for His Glory. There were many youth there that night, praising and worshipping God. Some were crying even the men (something most men do not do in public). I said, "Lord, if you ever raise me up to this level, I promise you all the Glory and honor." Second, the sweet presence of God made me weep.

On Friday (which was the last day of the crusade), Benny Hinn said that he was going to be praying for the

100

youth at the end of the service. As soon as he said that, I went as close as I could to the front.

A few minutes before the service ended, he said the magic words "I want all those under the age of twenty nine to come up to the altar so I can pray for you." I was hungry for the presence of the Lord and I was willing to do anything to get more of Him.

I quickly rushed to the front, pushing people out the way. I did not want anyone to stand in my way of receiving my miracle. Even though he called for people under twenty-nine, I saw people much older than twenty-nine running to the altar as well. I could not blame them because some of them were as hungry as I was.

Finally, after reaching the front of the line, I raised my hands and started worshiping God. I tried to get on stage where he was but I could not because of the crowd.

When the young people arrived in the front, he told everyone to grab a hold of someone's hands. He said, "I will pray for you and the power of God will fall on you".

At that point, I did not care if the person's hand I was holding had fungus growing in it; I wanted more of what he had. We grabbed each other's hands.

He started praying, "Father in the name of Jesus I pray that you will touch your young people, give them a hunger, and thirst for you, touch." Immediately when he said "Touch," the power of God knocked people down. Man, it was awesome!

Something amazing happened that night while on my way home. I felt the presence of God all over me. When I went home, I prayed and asked God to give me more of His presence. My hunger and thirst for God has never been the same.

Everyday I woke up seemed brighter and better. I felt closer to God than I had ever been. My life was changed from the touch of the Master's hand. The precious Holy Spirit met me in that arena and changed my life. He can do the same for you. The prerequisite for that special touch is hunger. The precious Holy Spirit touched me because I was hungry for Him.

God is looking for those that are hungry for His presence and not only for His blessings. Many people spend time with God only because they want something from Him. Your life will change when you start worshipping God for who He is.

He is real

The Holy Spirit is part of the Godhead that many people do not understand. They do not understand Him because they cannot see Him. In order to have a great relationship with the Holy Spirit, you have to understand who the Holy Spirit is. He is as real as you are. He wants to change you life today.

As I learn more about the Holy Spirit, I have come to understand the Person of the Holy Spirit much better. It is important that as believers we understand that the Holy Spirit is a *Person*, not an "it" or "thing."

Many people are so afraid of Him. The precious Holy Spirit wants to be your friend too. He is not here to harm you but to love you. He is the only Person that will accept you for who you are; why not give Him a chance? He is standing outside of your heart, waiting to get that invitation to come in. Please let Him in. I promise, He will not hurt you.

How do we know that He is a person? Well, here are some ways we know the Holy Spirit is a person rather than an "it" or a "thing."

1. He has an Intellect.

Can the Holy Spirit think? Can He reason and remember? Both of those are valid and fair questions to ask. According to God's word, He has those abilities, and as a Person, He has an intellect. Yes, that means as you and I are able to think and process information He too can do that. In fact, the Bible says He searches all things. "But God has revealed them to us through His Spirit. For the Spirit searches all things, yes, the deep things of God" (1 Cor. 2:10).

Unlike our knowledge, God's Spirit knowledge is infinite and infallible. His knowledge goes even further than that, in that He searches the depth and magnitude of the Father's plans. In addition, He shares the knowledge with us. "For what man knows the things of a man except the spirit of the man which is in him? Even so no one knows the things of God except the spirit of God" (v 11). As you can see from this passage, it is clear that the Holy Spirit not only reveals the truth, but He also *knows* the truth.

In the book of Romans, the scripture itself declares that the Holy Spirit has a mind: "Likewise the Spirit also helps in our weaknesses. For we do not know what we should pray for as we ought, but the Spirit Himself makes intercession for us with groaning which cannot be uttered. Now He who searches the hearts knows what **the mind of the spirit** *is*, because He makes intercession for the saints according to the will of God" (Romans 8:26-27, emphasis added).

While reading that verse, I noticed three things in this passage: First, the Holy Spirit *prays* for us. Second, He searches our hearts. Third, he has a mind ("mind of the Spirit"). The word "mind" here is a comprehensive word, which encompasses the ideas of though, feeling, and purpose. This is amazing. It blew my mind when I found out that the Holy Spirit had a mind just like you and me. Like many Christians, I knew of the Holy Spirit but not about Him.

Have you ever wanted to quote a scripture or recall something you learned or studied but had a hard time doing it, and then all of a sudden it came to your memory? The Lord Jesus made it clear when He promised that the Holy Spirit would "teach you all things, and *bring to your remembrance*" (John 14:26, emphasis added).

2. He has a will.

After Jesus Christ ascended into heaven, He placed the Holy Spirit in charge of the church. He has a will of His own and has decision-making responsibilities here on earth.

The apostle Paul said, "The same Spirit who works all things, distributing to each one individually *as He wills*" (1 Corinthians 12:11, emphasis added). Everyone working in the Kingdom of God is subject to the direction of the Holy Spirit as well. That is why Paul told the elders of the church at Ephesus: "The Holy Spirit has *made* you overseers" (Acts 20:28, emphasis added).

It is vital that as disciples of Christ, we stay in tune with the direction of the Holy Spirit.

3. He has emotions.

The Holy Spirit is not some unemotional entity, incapable of compassion or concern. Just like you and I have feelings and a heart, so does He. Here are two ways His emotions are expressed.

First, the Holy Spirit can love. Love is more than a characteristic of the Holy Spirit: it *is* His character.

Have you ever felt unloved and needed extra love? The precious Holy Spirit can give you that love. I will let you in on a personal secret of mine (do me one favor: please tell everybody). The Holy Spirit is my source of Love as well as other things. Whenever I feel unloved, or need more love, He is the only one I go to.

I cannot explain how wonderful it feels to be love by the Holy Spirit. Benny Hinn once said, "God *so loved me* that he sent His son. *His Son so loved me* that He died for me. And the *Holy Spirit so loved me* that He came and revealed the Lord Jesus to me. And the same Holy Spirit continues to love me and help me become more and more like the Lord Jesus."

Second, the Holy Spirit can be grieved. The Holy Spirit is tender, gentle, and loving and can easily be wounded. You mean the Holy Spirit can get hurt? Yes, emotionally He can. Jesus said, "*Grieved* by the hardness of their hearts" (Mark 3:5, emphasis added).

The word grieve means torment, cause sorrow, vex, offend, insult, or cause pain. The Holy Spirit has a tender heart that will easily weep for you and me. There are several ways to grieve Him. For example, you know of someone that needs Jesus. Every time you see them, something (which is actually someone) tells you to minister to them, but you keep saying later.

All Christians are guilty of that, including me. That tugging you feel in your heart is the precious Holy Spirit telling you that if you do not tell that person about Jesus, when they die, they are going to Hell. Let me share with you a story to make this point.

I had a friend who felt this tugging on is heart concerning his dad. His dad was sick and in the hospital. Even though his father knew about the Lord, he had not accepted Him as his personal Lord and Savior. He kept saying, "Later."

One day, while watching TV with his dad, he felt the Holy Spirit telling him to minister to him immediately. Therefore, he did. Because of his obedience to the Holy Spirit, his father accepted Jesus as his Lord and Savior. A week after accepting Jesus, his dad went home to be with the Lord. Great things happen when you are obedient to the Holy Spirit.

Is there someone in you life that the Lord wants you to share your faith with? If so, do not be disobedient, regardless of whom it is. I will be the first to tell you that ministering to your family is a very difficult thing to do. Nonetheless, the rewards are great.

4. He can speak.

While the believers at Antioch were worshipping the Lord, "*the Holy Spirit said*, 'Now separate to me Barnabas and Saul for the work to which I have called them" (Acts 13:2, emphasis added). When you worship, you invite His presence. That sets the stage for him to speak to *us* and *through us*. Not to say that He cannot speak any other time, but there is something special that happens when you begin worship. This is so because worship touches the heart of God. Anyone can praise, but not everyone can worship. True worship comes from the heart. If your heart is not right, then you cannot truly worship God.

"But the hour is coming, and now is, when the **true worshipers** will worship the Father in spirit and truth; for the Father is seeking such to worship Him. God is a Spirit: and they that worship him must worship him in spirit and in truth" (John 4:24, emphasis added).

The Holy Spirit not only speaks directly at us, he can also speak through us. David stated, "The Spirit of the Lord spoke through me," (2 Sam. 23:2, emphasis added).

Unlike the Old Testament days when God choose specific people to speak through, when Jesus Christ redeemed us it became possible for Him to speak through ordinary people like you and me. I pray that you will hear His voice and be obedient to it.

106

5. He can be insulted.

The word "Insult" here carries with it the idea of treating with utter contempt or arrogance. When we fail to appreciate the significance of Christ's death on the cross for us, we insult the Holy Spirit.

It is dangerous to remove the blood or to decrease the importance of Christ's sacrifice for us. When that happens, we close the door to the Holy Spirit and make room for Satan. If Christ did not go back to the heaven, the precious Holy Spirit would not have been available to us.

It is sad to know that there are churches that do not preach about salvation. Because of that, people perceive Christ only as a morally good person (which He is) and not as the savior. However, the privilege to accept Him in their hearts is never given.

Insulting the Holy Spirit results in losing his presence—something I never want to experience. In fact, I would rather have His presence than anything else in the world. David understood this concept when he said; "take not thy spirit from me" (Ps. 51:11).

6. *He can be lied to*

One of the commandments God gave Moses to give to Israel was "Do not lie" (Lev. 19:11). This was not only to help guide us, but it also be applies to God's Spirit. Lying to the Holy Spirit is something that I do not encourage. Let us look at a story from the Book of Acts 5 about lying to the Holy Spirit. This is the story about Ananias and His wife Sapphira.

"But a certain man named Ananias, with Sapphira his wife, sold a possession. And he kept back part of the proceeds, his wife also being aware of it, and brought a certain part and laid it at the apostles' feet. But Peter said, Ananias, why has Satan filled your heart to lie to the Holy

Spirit and keep back part of the price of the land for yourself? While it remained, was it not your own? And after it was sold, was it not in your own control? Why have you conceived this thing in your heart? You have not lied to men but to God.

Then Ananias, hearing these words, fell down and breathed his last. So great fear came upon all those who heard these things. And the young men arose and wrapped him up, carried him out, and buried him.

Now it was about three hours later when his wife came in, not knowing what had happened. And Peter answered her, Tell me whether you sold the land for so much? She said, yes, for so much.

Then Peter said to her, How is it that you have agreed together to test the Spirit of the Lord? Look, the feet of those who have buried your husband are at the door, and they will carry you out. Then immediately she fell down at his feet and breathed her last. And the young men came in and found her dead, and carrying her out, buried her by her husband."

We must be careful and never forget that He is also *God Almighty*!

I encourage you to get to know this wonderful person. You life will never be the same when you have an encounter with Him. He changed me; He can also do the same for you.

Chapter 16

Renewed

Something amazing happens when you spend time with the Precious Holy Spirit. You become empowered to overcome spiritual obstacles as well as life's ordinary obstacles. I hope that after reading this chapter, you will pray and ask God to give you a desire to spend more time in His presence. It will change your life forever.

A word of Hope and Encouragement

Repent therefore and be converted, that your sins may be blotted out, so that times of refreshing may come from the presence of the Lord. (Acts 3:19)

His Presence

Several things happen when you spend time in the Presence of God. Here are a few of them.

- It changes you
- It rejuvenates you
- It encourages you
- It changes your circumstance
- It guides
- It feels great

It changes you

Everyday, I strive to be more like Jesus. Spending time in the presence of God gets me closer to that goal. Have you ever wanted to change but you did not know how to? You have tried everything but nothing seems to work. Well, look no further; I have the answer you have been searching for—His presence.

Being in the presence of God shows you what you need to get right in your life, if only you will get on your knees and pray. There is a song I learned titled, "Change me." The writer said, "Change me into your image, Lord; into your likeness, Lord, change me. I want to be like you, be like you. Oh, Lord! Change me". There are things in our lives that are not pleasing to God and He wants to change us.

Change can be a good thing even though many people do not like it. If you are not willing to change for anyone else, please be willing to change for God. There are certain things that God will not do in our lives unless we allow Him to mold us.

"**In the year that King Uzziah died**, I saw the Lord sitting on a throne, high and lifted up, and the train of His robe filled the temple" (Is. 6:1, emphasis added).

The prophet Isaiah would not have been able to see the Glory of God if King Uzziah did not die. King Uzziah represents an area in our lives that needs deliverance. In order for God to make you, He first has to break you.

Look at David; he was the "apple of God's eye." David had Bathsheba's husband Uriah purposely killed in battle because David had impregnated her and did not want Uriah to find out. You can read the complete story in II Samuel 11.

However, in Psalm 51:1-14, David repented for what he did.

"Have mercy upon me, according to your loving kindness; According to the multitude of your tender mercies blot out my transgression. Wash me thoroughly from my iniquity, and cleanse me from my sin. For I acknowledge my transgression and my sin is ever before me. Against you, you only, have I sinned, and done this evil your sight that you may be found just when you speak, and blameless when you judge. Behold, I was brought forth in iniquity, and in sin my mother conceived me. Behold, you desire truth in the inward parts, and in the hidden part you will make me know wisdom. Purge me with hyssop, and I shall be clean; wash me, and I shall be whiter than snow. Make me hear of joy and gladness, that the bones you have broken may rejoice. Hide your face from my sins and blot out all my iniquities. Create in me a clean heart, O God, and renew a steadfast spirit within me. Do not cast me away from your presence, and do not take your Holy Spirit from me. Restore to me the joy of your salvation, and uphold me by your generous Spirit. Then I will teach transgressors your ways and sinners shall be converted to you. Deliver me from the guilt of bloodshed, O God of my salvation, and my tongue shall sing aloud of your righteousness."

Before moving forward, I want you to take a moment and ask the Holy Spirit to convict you of anything in your life that needs to be changed. You can pray, "Holy Spirit, please reveal to me anything in my life that's not pleasing before you. Change me into your image, Lord, into your likeness. I want to be like you." The Holy Spirit will show you something or remind you of something that He wants you to change.

It rejuvenates you

The presence of God always rejuvenates me. One day after school, I was tired. I went to my room and took a nap. After waking up, I took a shower and felt refreshed. That is how it is with the presence of God. It refreshes and encourages you.

Sometimes, we are so busy with our everyday life that we forget to take some time out and ask God for strength. Some people get grouchy, aggravated, and tired because they do not spend adequate time in the presence of God.

"He gives power to the weak, and to those who have no might He increases strength. Even the youth shall faint and be weary, and the young men shall utterly fall, but those who wait on the Lord shall renew their strength; they shall mount up with wings like eagles, they shall run and not be weary, they shall walk and not faint" (Isaiah 40:30, emphasis added). Let God renew your strength.

It encourages you

Everyone needs encouragement. However, sometimes we cannot always find people to encourage us. All we hear from people are the things we do wrong and seldom the things we do right. I know what it is like to have people telling you all the things wrong with you. You messed this up, you did this, and you did that.

Constantly hearing negative things about yourself gets you depressed. You feel unloved and unappreciated. You will be surprised how a simple hello can change someone's life.

There are people waiting to be encouraged by you, so please make it your responsibility to encourage someone, even if it is just asking them about their day, family, or work. Let them know that someone cares.

As much as people's encouragement might help you, God's encouragement helps you the more. There is nothing more exciting than being encouraged by God.

It guides you

Sometimes in life, we are faced with difficult decisions. God can help you to make the right decisions. He will not force anything on you. Are you confused about anything, or not sure? All you have to do is ask Him.

"If any of you lack wisdom, let him ask of God who gives to all liberally and without reproach, and it will be given to him." (James 1:5)

Are you graduating high school and are not sure of which college to attend? Are you already a college student struggling about what to major in? Maybe you just graduated college and are ready to settle down but you are not sure if the girl you are with is the one God wants you to marry? All these are decisions some of us have to make at one point or another. If you are not sure, pray about it.

It feels great

I cannot tell you how many times I have been in the presence of God and did not feel like leaving. I have learned that this type of presence comes when you pray continuously.

You too can have that kind of relationship with the Holy Spirit. Everyday I pray and ask God to give me more passion to seek Him. The more I do that, the more I enjoy His presence. There have been times that I went on my knees and said I will pray just for about five to ten minutes but ended up in prayer for hours. God's presence is sweeter than honey. I hope you too will experience that in your fellowship with God.

Chapter 17

Spiritual Warfare

The Apostle Paul informed us that our battles are not physical but spiritual. In order to win this battle, we need to be equipped for it. It is important that as believers we comprehend the seriousness of spiritual warfare. God's plan is not for any of His children to be bound in sin but to be free from sin.

A word of Hope and Encouragement

For we do not wrestle against flesh and blood, but against principalities, against powers, against the rulers of the darkness of this age, against spiritual hosts of wickedness in the heavenly places. Therefore take up the whole armor of God, that you may be able to withstand in the evil day, and having done all, to stand. (Eph. 6:10)

The armor of God

"Finally, my brethren, be strong in the Lord and in the power of His might. Put on the whole armor of God, that you may be able to stand against the wiles of the devil. For we do not wrestle against flesh and blood, but against principalities, against powers, against the rulers of the darkness of this age, against spiritual hosts of wickedness in the heavenly places. Therefore take up the whole armor of God, that you may be able to withstand in the evil day, and having done all, to stand" (Eph. 6:10-18).

We are soldiers in a war. In order to win, we are going to need the armor of God. The items of your equipment to fight this battle can be found in Ephesians 6:13-18, "Stand therefore, having your loins girt about with truth, and having on the breastplate of righteousness; and your feet shod with the preparation of the gospel of peace; Above all, taking the shield of faith, wherewith ye shall be able to quench all the fiery darts of the wicked. And take the helmet of salvation, and the sword of the Spirit, which is the word of God: praying always with all prayer and supplication in the Spirit, and watching thereunto with all perseverance and supplication for all saints."

The apostle Paul mentioned seven things we need to do in order to have on the complete armor of God. Let us take a closer look at each of them.

- The Belt of Truth
- The Breastplate of Righteousness
- The Shoe of the Preparation of the Gospel of Peace
- The Shield of Faith
- The Helmet of Salvation
- The Sword of the Spirit

116

- All prayer

The Belt of truth (v. 14)

During biblical times, men usually wore loose clothing that hung down below their knees. Before doing any strenuous work, they would gather up their loose garments above their knees and fasten it with a belt around their waist.

That is what we must do as well, gather up and fasten out of the way anything that would stop our freedom to follow Jesus. The "belt" that enables you to follow Jesus is God's word, and it is applied in a basic and practical way.

The Breastplate of Righteousness (v. 14)

Think of the breastplate as protecting your most critical and vulnerable area—your heart. If most of us can grasp this, it will save many people from getting their hearts broken. That is why the Bible says, "with the heart"— and not with the head—"one believes to righteousness" (see Rom. 10:10). We are cautioned to "**Guard** your heart because it's very precious" (see Prov. 4:23, emphasis added).

The Shoe of the Preparation of the Gospel of Peace (v. 15)

With a cell phone, you are able to move from one place to another; it is the same thing with your shoe. It makes you mobile. You must be available to God at any time or place to share the Gospel with those He put in your way. This will teach you how to make yourself available to God whenever, or wherever, and however He chooses to use you.

The Shield of Faith (v. 16)

A shield is use to protect your whole body. However, it is only effective when you learn how to use it. You too must learn to use your faith as a shield to protect your whole person—Spirit, soul, and body—from Satan's fiery darts. Not only will the shield protect you from the flaming darts, but it will also extinguish them.

The Helmet of Salvation (v. 17)

The helmet protects another vulnerable area—the head that is the mind. It is not safe riding a bicycle or motorcycle without a helmet because if you get in an accident, that helmet can save your life. That is why it is important to protect it. Satan will attack your mind more than any other part of your personality.

The Sword of the Spirit—the Word of God (v. 17)

Knowing the word of God is important. Having the Bible on your bookshelf or front steps will not protect you from being attack by Satan. God's word becomes a sword when you speak it through your mouth in faith. Do what Jesus did in Mathew 4 when Satan tempted him. He answered him back by quoting scriptures: "it is written". It is vital that we learn how to model after Jesus.

The Final Weapon— All Prayer (v. 18)

Prayer changes things. Through prayer, someone who lives far away in another continent or state can be healed. I have heard stories about people who prayed for their families, relatives, or friends from different countries and God answered their prayers. It takes discipline and maturity to learn to use such a powerful weapon. Never underestimate the power of prayer.

Chapter 18

Breakthrough

Sin does three primary things to you. First, sin takes you farther than you intend to go. Second, sin costs you more than you are willing to pay. Third, sin holds you longer than you are willing to stay.

Are you struggling with sexual purity? Do you need deliverance? If so, get ready to be saved. Today is the day that God wants to release you from the enemy's yokes and bondages.

A word of Hope and Encouragement

Hear, O Lord, when I cry with my voice! Have mercy also upon me, and answer me. When you said, "Seek My face," my heart to said to You, "Your face, Lord, I will seek." Do not hide Your face from me; Do not turn your servant away in anger; You have been my help; do not leave me nor forsake me, O God of my salvation. (Ps. 27:7-9)

Deliverance

Are you struggling with masturbation, lust, porn, or something else? There is no such thing as a big sin or little sin. Sin is sin regardless of how you look at it. God wants to set you free and make you pure and holy so that He can use you. His word says, "You shall be holy, for I the LORD your God am Holy (Lev. 19:2).

Holiness is a decision we must make as Christians. I know what it is like to struggle with sin and feel helpless. You do not have to feel helpless any longer; The Holy Spirit is going to help you. Get ready to receive your deliverance. I will show you some steps on how to be delivered from whatever you are going through. Before I do that, there is one thing to keep in mind. You must *will* to do this.

As human beings, if we do not want to do something and we do it anyway, it does not always work. However, if it does, it never lasts. This is serious. So please do not take this lightly.

The main reason I was delivered from porn, masturbation, and lusting is because I was tired of doing the same thing repeatedly, repenting for it, and going back to it. That was not true repentance. True repentance comes when you do something wrong, *genuinely* repent, and stay away from it.

God's plan is not for us to be in bondage. Jesus Christ wants to set you free. All you have to do is touch the hem of His garment and you shall be made whole. It is time you put the enemy under your feet, where he belongs. The devil has no right or authority over you. Jesus bought you at a price when He died on the cross. When Christ died on the cross, He died for your freedom as well.

I know what it feels like to be bound in sin. I also know what it feels like to be free from bondage. You can be set free and stay free, there are two ways you can do this.

You can have someone pray for you or praying for yourself. Keep in mind that depending on the severity of your addiction or bondage, certain deliverances can take place in your bedroom, car, or bathroom as you pray, while others need the help of a *spiritually mature* believer. This could be your pastor or someone you trust. It is advisable that you speak with your pastors first before doing anything.

Having someone pray for you

When I was delivered, my mom prayed for me. That was great because I had someone to encourage and support me. Some people need that extra encouragement. I did.

However, let me caution you again. It is imperative that you have someone spiritually mature and knowledgeable about deliverance. It could be your pastor or an intercessor. Demons are not toys, so do not play with them. The last thing is to get someone that is not mature and they both of you start freaking out when something happens. They may have to help calm you down so that no one gets hurt.

This may be unorthodox for some, which is normal. Nevertheless, sometimes to get what you want, you have to able to sacrifice everything.

Different things might happen to you while in the process of deliverance. I mentioned earlier that I was vibrating and screaming when I was being delivered. Do not be afraid if that happens to you.

We see an example of this in Mark 9:14-28, "And when He came to the disciples, He saw a great multitude around them, and scribes disputing with them. Immediately, when they saw Him, all the people were greatly amazed, and running to Him, greeted Him. And He asked the scribes, "What are you discussing with them?"

Then one of the crowd answered and said, "Teacher, I brought You my son, who has a mute spirit. And wherever it seizes him, it throws him down; he foams at the mouth, gnashes his teeth, and becomes rigid. So I spoke to your disciples that they should cast it out, but they could not.

He answered him and said, "O faithless generation, how long shall I be with you? How long shall I bear with you? Bring him to me." Then they brought him to Him. And when he saw Him, immediately the spirit convulsed him, and he fell on the ground and wallowed, foaming at the mouth.

So He asked his father, "How long has this been happening to him?" And he said, "From childhood. And often he has thrown him both into the fire and into the water to destroy him. But if You can do anything, have compassion on us and help us." Jesus said to him, "If you can believe, all things are possible to him who believes." Immediately the father of the child cried out and said with tears, "Lord, I believe; help my unbelief!" When Jesus saw that the people came running together, He rebuked the unclean spirit, saying to it, "Deaf and dumb spirit, I command you, come out of him and enter him no more!" Then the spirit cried out, convulsed him greatly, and came out of him. And he became as one dead, so that many said, "He is dead." But Jesus took him by the hand and lifted him up, and he arose."

The reason why that happened is that the evil spirit inside of the boy did not want to come out.

Praying for yourself

You can pray for yourself when you are struggling with cursing, lying, etc. Deliverance in this area does not require as much prayer as the story of the boy healed by Jesus in Mark 9. I believe that if you want to be delivered, you can be. After struggling with the battle of the eyes, I was tired and wanted to be free.

If you pray alone, here are the things you must do:

Affirm your faith in Jesus Christ

Here is what you say, "Lord Jesus Christ, I believe You are the son of God and the only way to God—that you died on the cross for my sins and rose again so that I might be forgiven and receive eternal life."

Humble Yourself:

"I renounce all pride and religious self-righteousness and any dignity that does not come from you. I have no claim on your mercy except that you died in my place." Keep in mind that God resists the proud, but give grace to the humble. That is why it is important for us to make ourselves humble before Him.

Confess your sins:

This is where you let it all out. Be honest! "I confess all my sins before you and hold nothing back. Especially I confess...."

Repent of all sins:

"I repent of all my sins. I turn away from them and I turn to You, Lord, for mercy and forgiveness."

Forgive:

If you want God to forgive you, you first have to forgive those that have hurt you. "I forgive all who have ever harmed or wronged me. I lay down all bitterness, all resentment, and all hatred. Specifically, I forgive...." As you do this, the Holy Spirit will bring specific things and people to you. Forgive them and let it go.

Get ready for your freedom:

You are about to be free from the bondage of the enemy. "Lord Jesus, I think you that on the cross you were made a curse, that I may be redeemed from every curse and inherit God's blessing. On that basis I ask you to release me and set me free to receive the deliverance I need."

Stand strong:

Do not give up but keep on pressing in. "I take my stand with You, Lord, against all Satan's demons. I submit to You, Lord, and I resist devil. Amen!"

Start rebuking:

"Now I speak to any demons that have control over me. [Speak freely to them]. I command you to go from me now. In the name of Jesus, I bind you!"

If you do this sincerely, God will set you free. "And it shall come to pass that **whoever calls** on the name of the Lord shall be save (Joel 2:32, emphasis added).

Congratulations! You are now a free person. Now that you are free, you have to learn how to stay free. It is much difficult to stay free than to get free. The next chapter will help you with that.

Chapter 19

Staying free

It is vital that when God delivers us from anything that we stay free. If we do not, the state we end up in will be worse than the one we were in before.

A word of Hope and Encouragement

Then Jesus said to those Jews who believed Him, "If you abide in My word, you are My disciples indeed. And you shall know the truth, and the truth shall make you free." They answered Him, "We are Abraham's descendants, and have never been in bondage to anyone. How can You say, 'You will be made free'?" Jesus answered them, "Most assuredly, I say to you, whoever commits sin is a slave of sin. And a slave does not abide in the house forever, but a son abides forever. Therefore if the Son makes you free, you shall be free indeed. (John 8:31-36)

Freedom in Jesus Christ

Maintaining your deliverance can be challenging at times. However, it is not impossible because "I can do all things through Christ who strengthens me" (Phil. 4:13). Here are some ways to help you maintain your deliverance and purity.

1. Get in the Word

It is important to study the word of God. There are several benefits of doing that. Here are just a few of them.

First, it draws you closer to God. In my walk with God, I have found several ways to get closer to God—prayer, fasting, and reading the Bible. The Bible teaches us that in order to get closer to God, we must "submit to God. Resist the devil and he will flee from you. Draw near to God and He will draw near to you" (James 4:7-8).

I once saw a T-shirt that said, "If God seems far, who moved?" God is unmovable, and always stable. He seems far only to those who do not seek Him diligently.

Second, it gives you a fresh revelation. When you spend time reading God's word, He reveals his plan for your future. "**No eye has seen, no ear has heard**, no mind has conceived what God **has** prepared for those who love Him" (I Corinthians 2:9, emphasis added). This is such an encouragement to know that God has not forgotten about us. He died so that you might have life and have it more abundantly (see John 10:10).

I love God's word because I do not have to depend on others to know His will for my life. You do not need anyone to interpret scriptures for you when you have the Holy Spirit. He will guide you and interpret it for you. Just ask Him.

Third, it equips believers for tough questions. Even though we do not have the answer to every question, we are encouraged to "study to show yourself approved."

However, many people do not do that. It is very saddening to see unbelievers who know the Bible better than Christians do. As Christians, we should be able to answer certain questions posed to us by unbelievers. Many Christians cannot answer basic fundamental questions because they are not taking God's word seriously enough.

Fourth, it encourages you. The word of God always encourages me. Whenever I feel like giving up, I can turn to Philippians 4:13 and say, "I can do all things through Christ who strengthens me." When the enemy is attacking me, I can let him know that, "*No weapon* formed against me shall prosper. And every tongue that rises against me in judgment you shall condemn" (Is. 54:17, emphasis added). Whenever I feel as if I am losing my spiritual battles, I let the enemy know that, "Greater is He [Jesus] that's in me than he [Satan] that's in the world" (1 John 4:4). When I forget about God's blessings and promises for my life, His word says, "Surely **goodness** and **mercy** shall follow me all the days of my life" (Ps. 23:6, emphasis added). "My God shall **supply all your** need according to His riches in glory by Christ Jesus" (Phil. 4:19, emphasis added).

I have used all these scriptures and more to combat doubt and discouragement from the enemy. These are just a few of them. There are many more. Check it out!

Fifth, it guides us. As people of God, there are times when we all need guidance and direction. Many people are looking for spiritual guidance. Unfortunately, most only get secular guidance. I would rather get spiritual guidance from a believer's perspective than from a non-believer's. What do you do when you need direction? Proverbs 3:5-6 has your answer, "**Trust** in the LORD with all your heart, and **lean not** on your own understanding; in **all your ways**

acknowledge Him, And He shall direct your paths"
(Emphasis added).

2. Become part of a church

Make sure that you find a good Bible-based church
that believes in the Birth, Death, and Resurrection of Christ.
This is an opportunity to get some of your questions
answered. This will help you draw closer to God. If you need
help finding a church home, pray and ask God to lead you.
He always does.

3. Develop healthy relationships

Hang around people who want the same thing out of
life as you do. Pray for God to send you Christian friends
and people that will love you and not be quick to judge you.
I thank God every day for the friends He sent me. Without
them, I would have made many mistakes, but with them, I
avoided more mistakes.

When dating, be careful who you choose as your
partner. The apostle Paul said, "Do not be unequally yoked
together with unbelievers. For what fellowship has
righteousness with lawlessness? And what communion has
light with darkness? And what accord has Christ with Belial?
Or what part has a believer with an unbeliever? And what
agreement has the temple of God with idols? For you are the
temple of the living God. As God has said: I will dwell in
them and walk among them. I will be their God, and they
shall be My people. Therefore come out from among them
and be separate, says the Lord. Do not touch what is unclean,
And I will receive you. I will be a Father to you, And you
shall be My sons and daughters, says the LORD Almighty"
(2 Cor. 6:14-17).

4. Be filled with the Holy Spirit

This is my favorite step. The Holy Spirit is my best friend and over the years, I learned to depend solely on Him.

In Joel 2:28 God said, "And it shall come to pass afterward that I will pour out My Spirit on all flesh; Your sons and your daughters shall prophesy, Your old men shall dream dreams, Your young men shall see visions. And also on My menservants and on My maidservants. I will pour out My Spirit in those days. And I will show wonders in the heavens and in the earth."

The Holy Spirit is for everyone, and not only for televangelists. God wants you to have an experience with His Spirit.

Living a Spirit-filled life is how believers should live. Here are a couple of functions of the precious Holy Spirit:

Counselor

"But the Counselor, the **Holy Spirit**, whom the Father will send in my name, will teach you all things and will remind you of everything I have said to you" (John 14:26).

Are you lost and needing to be found? Do you need advice about making the right decisions? Maybe you need a friend. The Holy Spirit is there for you. That is part of His job in our lives. A day does not go by without me talking to Him. There are times when I get upset and I am ready to give someone a piece of my mind. That is when I say, "Precious Holy Spirit, please help me stay calmed." If you need counsel, go to the Holy Spirit. He is the greatest counselor you will ever have.

Authority

You have the power to heal the sick, raise the dead, and cast out demons. That is all because of the power of the Holy Spirit. Most people do not understand how important the Holy Spirit is in our lives. People think of Him as an "it," rather than the "power source of the Godhead."

Jesus Christ would not have been resurrected from the dead without the Holy Spirit. It was only through the power of the Holy Spirit that He rose. "Not by might nor by power, **but by My Spirit**, Says the LORD of hosts" (Zech. 4:6, emphasis added).

We now have the Spirit of God living inside of us. We have the authority by Jesus to do what He did—heal the sick, raise the dead, and cast out demons. "All authority has been given to me in heaven and on earth" (Matt. 28:18).

Do you have a mountain in your life that does not seem to be moving? You can move that mountain with the help of the Spirit of God. Acts 1:8 "But you will receive power when the **Holy Spirit** comes on you" (emphasis added). You have the power to speak to your mountain to move. Trust God; speak to your mountain and see how powerful God is.

Chapter 20

Jesus, lover of my soul

Every day, I thank God for sending His only begotten Son to die for my sins. Words cannot express my gratitude. Having a personal relationship with Jesus has changed my life. Without Him, I am nothing. I hope that you too will make that personal decision to accept Him as your Lord and Savior.

A word of Hope and Encouragement

For God so loved the world that He gave His only begotten Son, that whoever believes in Him should not perish but have everlasting life. For God did not send His Son into the world to condemn the world, but that the world through Him might be saved. He who believes in Him is not condemned; but he who does not believe is condemned already, because he has not believed in the name of the only begotten Son of God. (John 3:16-18)

Do you know Jesus?

Today, people are often confused when asked about their faith. Many believers cannot answer basic questions about their faith because they do not know what they believe in. It is difficult to explain to someone about something that you are not sure about yourself. Unfortunately, that is what happens to many believers today. They talk the talk but cannot walk the walk. Do you know Jesus?

If you have a relationship with Jesus, when someone asks you about Him, you should be able to answer the question. For example, when someone asks you your name, you do not think about it for days or tell them you will get back to them when you have the answer. That is how it should be when someone asks you about your relationship with Jesus.

If you cannot tell people who Jesus is to you, that means He does not mean anything to you. I encourage you to find out for yourself who Jesus is; do not depend on your parents or anyone else to do that for you. Your friend's or your parent's salvation will not take you to Heaven.

Trusting Jesus

In all my years of walking with God, The Lord revealed an important thing to me about trust. There were times I trusted God only when I thought I knew what the outcome was going to be. I used to have a difficult time trusting God.

One night while fellowshipping with the Lord, I heard the Holy Spirit say, "Do you trust me?" I replied, "Of course I trust you, Lord." "If you trust me, why are you still worrying about your circumstances?" I was speechless.

The Lord is saying to His people, "Trust Me and I will come through for you. When have I ever let you down? If you say you trust me, why do you keep on doubting me?" Trusting God can be very challenging, especially if you have been hurt repeatedly by people.

It is difficult to become vulnerable to people because you are afraid of getting hurt. Do not let your hurts stop you from trusting God. He will never tell anyone your deepest secrets. You have to learn to trust Him with everything— your education, family, love life, and career. Proverbs 3:5-7 best describes this, "**Trust in the Lord with all your heart**, and lean not on your own understanding; in all your ways acknowledge Him, and He shall direct your path" (emphasis added).

Do not be wise in your own eyes. He does not want you to trust Him only in one area of your life but in every area.

When you start trusting God with every area of your life, He will make you stronger and better. Do not let doubt stand in the way of your blessings.

Following Jesus

We are told in Proverbs 3:5 to, "Trust in the Lord with all your heart, and lean not on your own understanding. In all your ways acknowledge Him, and He shall direct your path." In order to follow Jesus, there are some things to be mindful about.

1. Obedience (humility, trust)

God is looking for obedient people. It is difficult to work with or teach someone who is disobedient, someone who does not want to listen to anyone. Sad to say that is how we act towards God at times. With that kind of attitude, we will never be obedient to God. I have found some important things about obedience. Let us look at some:

a. Real obedience comes when you truthfully trust someone. It is difficult to obey someone that you do not trust. On the contrary, when you trust someone and know what their motives are towards you, it becomes much easier for you to obey them.

b. More doors of opportunity will be open to those who are obedient to God. Being obedient to your parents can be rewarding especially during your birthday or the holidays. Everything that comes out your mouth is, "yes mom" or "okay dad". We have to learn how to be obedient not only to God but also to our parents and guardians. Not only will God recompense you, but also it is, "Well pleasing to the Lord" (Colossians 3:20).

Successful individuals are usually obedient. They do not compare themselves to others. "Likewise you younger people, submit yourselves to your elders. Yes, all of you be submissive to one another, and be clothed with humility, for God **resists the proud**, but gives grace to the humble" (I Peter 5:5, emphasis added).

My daily prayer is for God to make me more obedient and humble. When people talk about me, I do not want them to say, "Mathew is full of himself, everything has to be his way." Rather, I want them to say, "Mathew's life reflects God's word."

c. You find genuine joy and peace. I cannot tell you how many times my disobedience to the Lord has caused me pain, headache, and depression; and the list goes on.

When God tells us to do something and we know in our hearts that it is definitely God's will, if we disobey Him the consequences will be great. Unfortunately, for me, I had to learn this the hard way.

As I mentioned earlier, I played sports in high school. I remember while getting ready for a soccer game, the Holy Spirit told me, "Don't play." Nevertheless, I wanted to play because I knew that there were going to be hot girls there and I wanted to impress them. Therefore, I said, "What's the worst that could happen? It's just a soccer game."

One minute before the game was over; the other team had the ball coming toward our goal to score. I was the striker and I had to defend them. As I went up to defend them from scoring, my ankle somehow collided with the shin of the other player. I felt as if I was hit with a football helmet on my ankle. I acted as if everything was fine so that my coach would allow me to play the next game.

I did not feel pain immediately after the game. When I woke up the following day, I had to be rushed to the emergency room because my ankle was swollen to almost the size of a tennis ball. My ankle is much better now. However, I have to be extremely careful when playing around. Because of my disobedience, my athletic career was over even before it started.

2. Don't lean on your own understanding

a. Our knowledge is limited, fallible, and sometimes erroneous. The apostle Paul said, "For we know in part" (1 Cor. 13:9). It is important for us not to depend on how much we know and can prove. Only God's knowledge is unlimited, infallible, and error free. Learn to depend on Him instead of you.

b. Be enlightened by God's words and be led by His Spirit. "But you are not in the flesh but in the Spirit, if indeed the Spirit of God dwells in you. Now if anyone does not have the Spirit of Christ, he is not His. And if Christ is in you, the body is dead because of sin, but the Spirit is life because of righteousness. But if the Spirit of Him who raised Jesus from the dead dwells in you, He who raised Christ from the dead will also give life to your mortal bodies through His Spirit who dwells in you" (Rom. 8:9-11).

c. Pray for wisdom. "If any of you lacks wisdom, let him ask of God, who gives to all liberally and without reproach, and it will be given to him" (James 1:5).

A man was once told, "You are very knowledgeable, but you always want to learn more." His reply was, "The older I get, the more I realize how little I know."

3. In all thy ways, acknowledge Him

a. In everything we do, we should acknowledge God as Lord, and His will as our supreme desire. Have you ever been acknowledged by people for doing something great?

I once was involved in a major drama production at my church. At the end of the play, there was a long line of kids coming to get my autograph. I felt special and I was honored that people wanted to get my autograph. It felt great to hear people say, "That was a fantastic job you did" or "Your parents must be proud of you".

God is a jealous God. (See Exodus 20:5.) He wants us to recognize Him in everything we do and to let people know that without Him, it is impossible to accomplish anything. When we do this, He promises to direct our path. He will lead us to His will for our lives, remove all obstacles, and enable us to make the right decisions.

b. Look to Him for direction. Before getting excited about anything, pray about it. "Be anxious for nothing, but in everything by prayer and supplication, with thanksgiving, let your requests be made known to God" (Philippians 4:6)

"The next award is for best performance. The award goes to…" Before the announcer could speak the winner's name, John stood up, jumping, shouting, and saying, "Hallelujah, hallelujah, thank you Jesus I won, I won."

Unfortunately, he did not win, someone else did. It can be embarrassing at times to get too anxious. Do not be too anxious about anything but rather take things to God in prayer.

What is Salvation?

A judge had a disobedient son who was always getting into trouble with the law. People came to him from everywhere because they received justice at his court.

Unfortunately, a day would come when this judge would have to make the toughest decisions he ever made.

One day, a young man was brought into his courtroom for coming a crime. To the judge's surprise, it was his son. Because he was a fair judge, he had to be fair and give his son the punishment he deserved, which was to pay a certain amount of money or else go to jail for life.

As the police walked his son out the courtroom, the judge stopped them. He reached in his pocket, took out his wallet, and paid the money his son owed. That is what Jesus did when He died on the cross for us.

"For God so **loved** the world that **He gave** His only begotten son, that whosoever believes in Him would not perish but have **everlasting life**" (John 3:16, emphasis added). God send Jesus to die on the cross so that you and I can have "everlasting life" (See John 10:10).

You might think that God would never forgive you because of the things you have done in the past. That is not true because, "**All have sinned** and fallen short of the glory of God" (Romans 3:23, emphasis added). This means that every man and woman born after Adam and Eve is born a sinner. Because of that, we deserve to die.

"For the wages of sin is death, but the gift of God is eternal life through Jesus Christ our Lord (Romans 6:23). No one is perfect. I have done many things that are not pleasing to God. However, when Jesus Christ came on the earth, He died for our sins because of His love for us. "But God demonstrates his own love for us in this: **While we were still sinners, Christ died for us**." (Romans 5:8, emphasis added)

All the things you did in the past can be forgiven when you accept Jesus Christ as your personal Lord and savior. He can wipe away your past regardless of how bad you think it is.

Sin separates us from God. Moreover, to get to God, we have to go through Jesus. Sin is missing the mark. In the old days, when an archer used his bow and arrow to shoot at a target, when he missed, they said he "sinned"—he missed the mark.

Is your life full of drama? Do you need peace and joy? Are you confused on where to go with your life and need direction? This is your opportunity to surrender to Jesus. If you think that Satan cares about you, he does not.

- Satan wants you to become drug dealers, prostitutes, murderers, and crack heads. (see John 10:10)

- Jesus wants you to become lawyers, doctors, teachers, and entrepreneurs. (See Jeremiah 29:11)

- Satan wants to take away your peace and replace it with pain, anger, and hopelessness. (see 1 Peter 5:8)

- Jesus wants to take away your pain, anger, and hopelessness and replace it with righteousness, peace, and joy. (See Matthew 11: 28-30)

- Satan wants to take away your future and make it an illusion. (See James 4:7)

- Jesus wants to take your dream and make it a reality. (See John 14:6)

138

- Satan wants to take your mind and replaces it with confusion. (See Ephesians 4:27)

- Jesus wants to take away that confusion and replace it comprehension. (See Proverbs 3:5-6)

- Satan wants to take away your joy and replace it with addiction. (See 2 Corinthians 2:11)

- Jesus wants to take that addiction and replace it with conviction. (See Psalms 51:10)

Whose side are you on?

If you want to be saved, all you have to do is, "**Confess** with your mouth the Lord Jesus and **believe** in your heart that God has raised Him from the dead, you will be saved" (Romans 10:9, emphasis added).

People do not die and go to hell because of sin; rather, people die and go to hell because they refuse God's gift of salvation. Will you accept Jesus as your personal Lord and savior? Tomorrow is not promised to anyone. This could be your last opportunity. Repeat this prayer:

"Heavenly Father, your word says all have sinned, including me, and because of sin, I deserve to die. I believe that your Son Jesus died on the cross for my sins and on the third day, He rose from the dead. Come into my heart, Lord Jesus, and be the Lord of my life. I surrender everything in my life over to you from this day. In Jesus' name, the one who died so that I might have life. Amen."

Welcome to the kingdom of God. You made the right decision, something you will cherish for eternity. There is a huge celebration in heaven when you accept Jesus as your Lord and savior.

"There is **rejoicing** in the presence of the angels of God over one sinner who repents" (Luke 15:10, emphasis added). Heaven is rejoicing for you. I can hear the angels cheering for you, "You did it. We have been waiting for you. Welcome to the family of God. We love you."

"If any man be in Christ, he is a **new creation**: **old things are passed** away; behold **all things are become new**." (2 Cor. 5:17, emphasis added). You are new as new as can be. Go and tell what Jesus has done for you.

Use Me Lord

I hope that you had as much fun reading this book as I did writing it. I hope that something was said that made you want to draw closer to God, or re-examine your walk with God. If we want to see the move of God in our generation as well as our nation, it has to start with us. Let us learn how to love, respect, and care for each other. "You shall love your neighbor as yourself" (Matt. 19:19)

It is time for the body of Christ to unite and stop pointing fingers at each other. We cannot expect the world to come to us if all they see among us is strife and division. Learn to "love your neighbor as yourself." The songwriter said it best:

"I need you, You need me

We are all a part of God's Body

Stand with me

Agree with me

We are all a part of God's Body

It is His will

That every need be supplied

You are important to me

I need you to survive

I pray for you

You pray for me

I love you, I need you to survive

I will not harm you

With words from my mouth

I love you I need you to survive"

Go impact the world for Jesus. In order to do that, we have to do it one person at a time. To influence the world for Jesus, you must first let Him influence you.